Celebrating Familie

Celebrating Families

Ideas and activities to help
your family grow in faith

Diana and Lawrence Osborn

Illustrated by Olga Marks

First published in Great Britain 1995
Society for Promoting Christian Knowledge
Holy Trinity Church
Marylebone Road
London NW1 4DU

Biblical quotations are taken from the *New International Version*, copyright ©
1973, 1978, 1984 by the International Bible Society. Published by Hodder &
Stoughton.

British Library Cataloguing-in-Publication Data
A catalogue record for this book is available from the British Library

ISBN 0–281–04824–X

Typeset by Wilmaset Ltd, Birkenhead, Wirral
Printed in Great Britain by
The Cromwell Press, Melksham, Wiltshire

For our children, Angela, Joanne and Steven

Contents

ACKNOWLEDGEMENTS

It would be impossible to list all the people who have played a part in bringing this book into being. This is simply because the material which forms the substance of the book has evolved gradually over the years as our family has grown. We have picked up ideas from family, friends, other books and adapted and incorporated them into our own way of being a family.

Nevertheless, there are a number of people whom we would like to thank for specific help in the preparation of this book:

Julie Anderson for her advice about banner-making and the original designs for the banners illustrated in this book;

Graham and Jackie Cray for their helpful advice about music in family worship;

Janet Dix for her suggestions about seasonal flower arrangements;

Olga Marks for her friendship as well as her illustrations.

Introduction

A question that has exercised us since before our first child was born is 'What makes our family distinctively Christian?'

In our experience, many Christian parents have similar questions. How can we share our faith with our children? How can we help them grow in faith? How can we help each other grow in faith? How can we so structure our lives together that visitors to our home will encounter an attractive model of family life that bears witness to our Christian faith?

The traditional answer to such questions has been family prayer. In some Christian circles this has become something of a moral imperative, backed up by slogans such as 'The family that prays together, stays together'.

The words 'family prayer' conjure up images of large Victorian families sitting silently as father reads at length from an enormous Bible, offers a mini-sermon and leads the household in prayer. They can also generate a tremendous amount of guilt as people struggle to reconcile the demands of such a time-consuming model with the demands of a busy modern lifestyle. Then there is the boredom factor: children today are simply not used to sitting still for fifteen or twenty minutes with relatively little sensory input.

Surveys suggest that most families simply abandon the struggle. Figures show that only 5% of professing Christian families in North America have any kind of regular family worship.

What is to be done? For the past decade we have been collecting ideas to make our own family prayers more enjoyable and to enrich our life together through worship and celebration. We have compiled a wide range of practical ideas for family traditions, celebrations, prayers and worship. Some have been drawn from our own experience. We have borrowed others from friends and their families. Yet more we have adapted from a variety of Christian traditions, both old and new.

The result is a recipe book for family celebrations rather than a rule book to be followed slavishly. For one thing it would be impractical to do everything we suggest. The ideas are intended to cover a wide range of ages and abilities (we began collecting them when our eldest daughter was born and she is now ten). Some will be beyond the capacity of very young children. Others will seem embarrassingly simple to older children. In our family we tend to dip into the A4 file that formed the main source for this book; one year we may do this, another year we may do that. We have found some ideas more helpful than others. Almost certainly you will find different sets of ideas helpful. Feel free to pick and choose. The point of the book is to provide ideas rather than a total programme for Christian family life!

This may still seem a bit daunting, particularly if you are starting from scratch with a family which already has a well-established routine. Recently a friend of ours in just such a situation asked us for just one thing she could do each week to make Sunday special. Why not start like that? Or, if even that seems too difficult, why not begin by picking out one or two ideas to give a Christian flavour to one of the major festivals of the year?

Chapter 1 deals in general terms with family prayer. The rest of the book can be divided into two main parts, reflecting different aspects of our experience of time. Chapters 2 to 8 focus on the recurring cycle of the seasons and the church year, including the traditional Christian festivals. You need not belong to a Christian tradition that emphasizes the church year to find useful ideas in these pages.

Chapters 9 and 10 recognize that there is more to our experience of time than the annual cycle; that, as individuals and families, we grow and change with the passage of time. In them we explore ways in which we can celebrate the various stages of life within the family.

We hope the suggestions we have made will increase your enjoyment of family celebrations.

1
Day by Day

WHY FAMILY PRAYERS?

Not just talk

There are many different ways of understanding prayer. But all forms of Christian prayer have one thing in common: they are all about communication with God. Prayer is the way we express our relationship with God. In prayer we give ourselves to God, expressing our joys, our sorrows, our anxieties, our fears, our thoughts, our feelings, our experiences, and our intuitions.

If prayer is communication, it cannot just be us talking to God. Communication must be two-way. It is a dialogue not a monologue. So prayer is also about listening to God. Over the centuries, Christians have heard God speak to them in many different ways: through the words of the Bible; through other Christians (especially, though by no means exclusively, through preaching); through the workings of their own soul (their conscience, their reason, dreams, visions); and through the natural world.

We may extend this further. Prayer is all the many ways in which our relationship with God can grow. It is instructive to compare our relationship with God and our relationships with those around us, not least the members of our family. Do we just talk *at* our friends and loved ones in the hope that this will be sufficient to make our relationship grow? No, of course not. We take an interest in those we love. We listen to what they have to say to us. We notice things about them. We go out of our way to learn as much as we can about them. We work and play together. We give them gifts.

Clearly, if prayer is about developing our relationship with God, we should not be content with talking at him. We should be using our imaginations and taking risks to find new ways of expressing our love and hear God expressing his love.

Mutual friends

We often think of our relationship with God as exclusive; as something private, between him and me. But such private spiritualities are a peculiar feature of our individualistic culture. The writers of the New Testament saw things very differently. For them, every individual Christian was an important part of the body of Christ. The author of the Letter to the Hebrews advises, 'Let us not give up meeting together, as some are in the habit of doing, but let us encourage one another – and all the more as you see the Day approaching' (Heb. 10.25).

We recognize that the author of Hebrews was speaking to the Church. In his culture, families would have met together as a matter of course. Family prayers would have been the norm whether the family was Christian, Jewish or pagan. In our culture many families never meet! We need to be reminded that the body of Christ can be expressed by as few as two or three gathering together: the family can and should be an expression of the body of Christ as it meets together to worship.

One of the benefits of family prayers is obvious and often commented on. We are often reminded that as parents we have the primary responsibility for the spiritual development of our children. Sending them to Sunday school is not enough. Christian spirituality is about the whole of life, not just about Bible stories and choruses on a Sunday morning. Regular family prayers allow us to model our relationship with God for our children. That is quite a challenge! Children are very adept at spotting discrepancies between what we say and what we do.

More than a collection of individuals

It is not enough, though, to see family prayers merely as a covert way of teaching children about God. Another answer to the question, 'Why family prayers?' has to do with the fact that the family is more than a collection of individuals who happen to share the same name or the same house. It has a corporate identity which is more than just the sum of the individuals who make it up.

We pray individually because we want to grow in our individual relationships with God. We want God to use all the available lines of communication to transform us so that our lives are a clearer expression of our faith.

Family prayers, on the other hand, symbolize our commitment to being more than just individuals sleeping under the same roof. Furthermore, they express our desire to see God working in us, not just as individuals but as a family.

Family portrait

What do you think of your family? Where would you put yourself in relation to other family members? Where is God in it all? It may be helpful to think about questions like this as you approach the issue of family prayers.

One way of exploring these questions is to ask each member of the family to draw a picture of the family. Self-conscious adolescents and grown-ups might prefer to draw a diagram insead. Ask them to show on the portrait or diagram where they are in relation to the rest of the family. Examination of these pictures may reveal expectations or fears that might not otherwise be expressed.

WAYS AND MEANS

General principles

In creating family prayer times and celebrations certain general principles should be borne in mind.

1. *Be flexible*. Families are dynamic, constantly changing as the members grow and change. We need to reflect those changes in our family prayers. What is appropriate for a family with toddlers is quite different from what might be appropriate for a family where the children range from toddlers to teenagers. And, before and after children, husband and wife are still a family: what is appropriate for them as a couple will be different again.

    Similarly we must adapt our prayers and celebrations to the needs and gifts of the individuals in our own family. In our family life music is an important feature, and this is reflected in our prayers.

    Another aspect of flexibility is making the most of the opportunities that arise. Because families are never entirely predictable we need to be able to adapt our prayers to unexpected developments. Our schedule should never be so rigid that it is unable to cope with family illness, major events or the absence of individual members. Paul commended the practice of learning to pray at all times. Equally there may be times when the family is together but not doing anything. Why not use such times for prayer? Car journeys are a good example: modern praise tapes and Christian stories are a good standby for fending off the monotony of long journeys or hours in traffic jams.

The need for flexibility is one reason why this cannot be a rule book. What works for our family or the other families we know may not work for your family. Like recipes in a cookery book, the ideas we offer here are for you to try. You may like them as they are. You may want to modify them (as you might alter the seasoning or ingredients in a recipe). You may discover that particular ideas do not work with your family. Or you may know without trying them that members of your family will be allergic to some of these suggestions.

2. *Keep it simple*. One of the secrets of successful family prayers is to keep such times fairly simple.

We live in a relatively informal culture. By and large we are not familiar or comfortable with complex rituals (except perhaps as spectators). Thus the Victorian model of family devotions, with father effectively reproducing in miniature a church service, is no longer appropriate.

Simplicity is particularly important for young children. (When our children were toddlers we discovered by trial and error that they did not find variety helpful.) Pre-schoolers cannot read so they have to memorize any songs or set prayers you use. They also appreciate the security of a familiar pattern. Be prepared for a certain amount of monotony: we found ourselves singing 'If I were a butterfly' every

evening for a couple of years because that is what our children wanted! On the other hand, there are few things more refreshing than the heartfelt prayers of a toddler.

But simplicity and repetition are helpful for grown-ups as well. With a simple pattern you may find it easier to concentrate on the point of what you are doing rather than wondering what is happening next.

3. *Keep it real.* Reality or honesty is not unrelated to the previous point. A very elaborate ritual prayer time will probably seem quite artificial and unrelated to real life for most children nowadays. They simply do not encounter such formality in everyday life at home or school. What impression do we create if we present them with a devotional time which is unlike anything else they ever experience? Do we unwittingly imply that God is unconnected with the rest of life?

Children also tend to be sensitive to hypocrisy. They will soon realize the truth if we put family prayers on simply for their benefit. Will they get the message that 'prayer is for kids' from our attitude to family prayers?

Creating a prayer space

Many Christians find it helpful to set aside a particular place for their private prayers. We know some who have turned spare bedrooms into private chapels. Others may choose a corner of a room that is also used for other purposes. Still others have a favourite place out of doors.

Such a practice may also be helpful for family prayers. It is not that we need a particular holy place where we can meet God. But we may benefit from a location where we are not likely to be distracted from praying and where the furnishings and decorations help rather than hinder our prayers.

Some people find that a visual image helps them to concentrate on praying. It may be a cross or an icon or other religious picture. Or we may use photographs of people for whom we want to pray.

Another possiblity would be to make a banner to decorate (and define) our worship space. Banners have become increasingly popular as a simple way of decorating churches. But why restrict them to churches? They are simple to make and can be a powerful visual aid to worship.

Banner-making

Begin by selecting a suitable piece of background material (anything that does not fray easily). Stitch hems and fold the top edge over to make a channel to take a length of dowel. Unless the banner is very large it won't need a pole across the bottom as well.

Decide on the wording and visual symbols. It is better to keep these fairly simple (at least, to begin with). These can be created in a variety of ways, but our personal preference is for cutting them from coloured felt. This material has the double advantage that it can be glued on to the banner and it doesn't fray.

Thread the dowel through the loop at the top and tie a length of string to each end to hang it.

Throughout this book you will find illustrations of simple banners which are suitable for use at home. Some of them have removable symbols You can make these by cutting out two copies of the motif.

Stick or stitch velcro strip to the back of one copy and sew the two together. The resultant image can be stiffened with card or stuffed to create a three-dimensional effect.

If the idea appeals to you, you could gradually build up a collection of seasonal banners. They are also suitable for special occasions such as birthdays. One banner-maker even made one to brighten up the hospital room of her terminally-ill father.

In our home we simply gather in the sitting-room for family prayers and we light a candle on the coffee table to act as a focal point (and a reminder that Christ, the Light of the World, is in our midst as we pray). On the other hand, in the mornings we simply pray in our bedroom: our bed has become a prayer space.

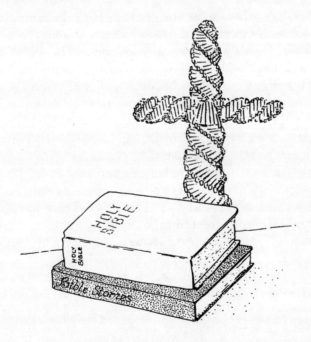

If a room or part of a room is set apart for regular prayer we may want to have all relevant books near at hand: Bibles, story-books, prayer books, hymn and chorus books (or whatever we use).

Music may also be helpful in creating a prayer space. It can serve to mask distracting noises from outside. More importantly the choice of music may affect the atmosphere we create: we may choose music that is suggestive of praise or music that evokes a quieter, more reflective mood.

Let's say grace

One possible time for family prayers is around the meal table. In Jewish and Christian families alike it is traditional to give thanks to God for the meal. In some traditions, this has been considerably elaborated so that the entire meal becomes an act of worship (as in the Jewish Passover Seder) or is permeated by devotional reading (as in some evangelical and Roman Catholic traditions).

The reason for using family meals as the focal point of family prayers is that for millennia the shared meal has been central to the establishment and strengthening of personal relationships. Those with whom our ancestors customarily shared their food were their nearest and dearest. The camp fire was also the place where the culture would be passed on to the next generation as story-tellers and musicians entertained and educated their fellows.

The Bible shares this almost universal emphasis on the importance of table fellowship. For example, the Gospels make a point of recording the complaints that Jesus ate with outcasts and sinners. By eating with them he identified himself with them in a way that scandalized 'decent folk'. The New Testament even describes our relationship with Jesus in these terms: 'I stand at the door and knock. If anyone hears my voice and opens the door, I will come in and eat with him, and he with me' (Rev. 3.20). Similarly, the object of the Christian hope is frequently portrayed as a meal: the marriage feast of the Lamb.

The importance of eating together can also be seen in the history of Christian worship. Our eucharist or communion service originated in the context of a common meal (1 Cor. 11.17–34). There has also been a recurring tendency, over the centuries, for groups of Christians to share common meals. Thanksgiving feasts were popular with the Puritans. Today we see it in the church supper or parish lunch.

Prayers of thanksgiving before (or perhaps after) common meals remind us that God is the unseen host at all our meals. God has not only provided us with the food we are able to enjoy but is present as we eat and talk together: God is an integral part of the community which is being strengthened by the meal (whether it is a harvest lunch, a housegroup supper, or family dinner).

Some graces

Graces (or prayers of thanksgiving) may be formal or informal, sung or spoken. Perhaps, if your imagination is up to it, they may be acted out or mimed!

Blessed art thou, O Lord our God, King of the Universe,
who bringest forth bread from the earth.

(Traditional Jewish blessing over bread)

Leader: The Lord gives food to the hungry and sets the captives
free.   *(Ps. 146.7)*
Leader: Let us give thanks to the Lord our God.
All: It is right to give him thanks and praise.
Leader: God our Saviour, we thank you for your love to us, for the
food you have provided, and for your command to share our
bread with the hungry and the stranger.[1]

Bless, O God, this food to our use and us to your service, and make us
ever mindful of the needs of others; through Jesus Christ our Lord.
Amen.

Blessed are you, O Lord God, Creator of the Universe, for you give us
food to sustain our lives and make our hearts glad; through Jesus
Christ our Lord. Amen.

Lord, help us to eat simply that others may simply eat.

(adapted from the motto of the Lifestyle Movement)

Bless us, O Lord, and let our food strengthen us to serve you, for
Christ's sake. Amen.   *(adapted from the New England Primer)*

Singing grace. Our children's favourite sung grace is an adaptation of a
popular chorus, 'Thank you, Lord, for this fine day' (JP 232)[2]. The
beauty of this grace is that you can substitute all sorts of things for
'this fine day'. When we sing it, the children often take turns and try
to thank God for everything they can see on the meal table. Other
favourites include the Doxology, 'Praise God from whom all blessings
flow' (JP 199, MP 557) and:

Thank you for the world so sweet,
Thank you for the food we eat.
Thank you for the birds that sing,
Thank you, God, for everything. Amen.

Ready for bed

Another popular time for family prayers is as part of the bedtime routine. Again, this may conjure up Victorian images of the child kneeling beside the bed saying 'God bless Mummy, God bless Daddy, God bless Aunty Flo . . .' Yet the end of the day is a good choice for family prayers. Generally bedtime is less rushed than early morning. It is a good time for looking back on the past day, giving thanks for what has been good, saying sorry for the bad things, thinking about what has happened today or is about to happen tomorrow and sharing it all with God.

When our eldest child was born we began a routine of giving her a blessing at bedtime. That tradition has been continued and extended to her younger brother and sister. As they grew older we gradually elaborated on that, introducing other prayers, Bible stories and songs. Eventually our family prayers outgrew their setting and we moved them downstairs.

Our daily pattern

We have retained the brief bedtime blessing for the children and sing the Lord's Prayer with them when they are in bed. However, family prayers now take place in the sitting-room immediately before the younger children go to bed. These are prayers for *all* the family since our work patterns enable both of us to be present much of the time. The pattern is a simple hymn-prayer sandwich.

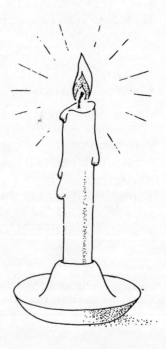

Prayers begin with the lighting of a candle.

Song: We generally use *Mission Praise* (simply because that is what
             our local church uses and the children are increasingly
             familiar with its contents).

Prayers: Every member of the family has the opportunity to say one
             or two *brief* prayers. This will usually be either giving thanks
             for something that has happened or praying about immedi-
             ate needs.

Song

Reading: We usually read a Bible story. When the children were
             younger the Palm Tree Bible stories were a particular
             favourite. More recently we have worked through *Cliff
             Richard's Favourite Bible Stories*
             (Conran Octopus, 1993) and the
             Lion Children's Bible (Lion,
             1981). Sometimes, for a change,
             we may read some other story
             with a clear religious theme (e.g.
             we recently serialized *The Family
             Pilgrim's Progress* (Scripture
             Union, 1983)).

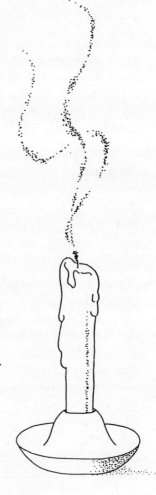

Song: We have three songs simply
             because we have three children
             and they all like to have their
             choice (though sometimes they
             let us choose).

Grace: 'May the grace of our Lord Jesus
             Christ, and the love of God and
             the fellowship of the Holy Spirit
             be with us now and forever.
             Amen.' (*said by all, holding hands*)

The candle is extinguished.

The children go upstairs to get ready for bed.
This is often accompanied by the singing of
'We are marching in the light of God', a
Christian chorus from South Africa
(Wildgoose Publications, 1990), or 'You
shall go out with joy' (MP 796, SOF 640).

We are not suggesting this as a pattern to be copied by other families. It is simply what has evolved in our family over the years and we expect it to go on changing as the children grow older. The important thing is to find out what will work for your family now.

DIY family prayers

What are the essential ingredients for family prayers? Probably these will differ from family to family. The example of our own family prayers includes several of the basic elements: prayers, a reading, songs, visual symbols. What would you want to add? Is there anything you would drop? How would you alter the elements that we have included?

- *Music*: Some families might feel more comfortable dropping this altogether. Others might prefer to use tapes or records.

- *Reading*: We use Bible stories and read for several minutes. Others might prefer a very brief reading from the Bible. Traditional evangelical family prayers would probably include a mini-sermon or comment on the passage that has been read. You may feel that something of that sort is appropriate or you may prefer to allow each family member to comment briefly on their reaction to the reading.

- *Prayers*: There are many ways in which this element could be altered. For example, the content might be varied, putting more emphasis on intercession or praise. Another possibility would be to use set prayers from a prayer book (e.g. Michael Botting offers a monthly cycle of set prayers and brief readings specifically for family use in his book *Prayers for All the Family* (Kingsway, 1993). Lion publishes several collections of prayers which are very suitable for family use.

- *Continuity and variety*: We live in a culture which sets great store by change. Look at any modern television programme and you will notice that it breaks down into units which are unlikely to last longer than two minutes. Teachers are trained to work within the attention span of their students rather than to stretch that attention span. The result is that many people (adults and children alike) find it hard to concentrate on any one activity for more than a very short period. This implies that if you want to spend a substantial amount of time on any one aspect of family prayers, you would be best to build up to that goal gradually.

  On the other hand, you may well find that there are recurring features which members of your family come to expect of family prayers. Such continuities can be helpful. They form a familiar pattern which helps us settle down to the business of praying. Too much variety may make family prayers more entertaining but it could detract from the real business which is to worship God.

As we pointed out earlier, very young children need the security of a simple repetitive structure. But children grow up; families change in composition as children are born or lodgers are welcomed, as people die or leave home. Families are dynamic and family prayers have to reflect that. This implies that you should not seek a single unchanging pattern of family worship. The best advice we can give is to experiment until you find the pattern that works for your family but be prepared to alter that pattern as circumstances change.

If we recognize the need to be adaptable we are more likely to notice the early warning signs telling us that it is time to alter what we are doing. Ideally we should welcome constructive criticism from every member of the family, allowing our prayer times together to reflect where we are as individuals and as a family. However, younger children may not be able to express dissatisfaction verbally. Instead we have to deduce it from signs of boredom (or embarrassment).

Rise and shine!

Early morning is a traditional time for prayers. Many Christians like to start the day with God. This is often the time chosen for the traditional quiet time.

However, it may not be the best time for family prayers. With children to get ready for school and husband and/or wife going out to work, the morning in many households is a time of rushing about. It is certainly not conducive to everyone sitting down together for family prayers!

For us, early morning is still the preferred time for individual devotions. It is not a matter of either individual or family prayers but 'both/and'. We say morning prayers together before we get out of bed and at various points in the morning routine the children do their daily Bible notes.

Waking prayers

Lord, you have watched over me, and put your hand on my head, during the long, dark hours of night. Your holy angels have protected me from all harm and pain. To you, Lord, I owe life itself. Continue to watch over me and bless me during the hours of day.

(*Jacob Boehme*)

Bless to me, O God,
     Each thing my eye sees;
Bless to me, O God,
     Each sound my ear hears;
Bless to me, O God,
     Each smell that reaches my nose;
Bless to me, O God,
     Each taste that touches my tongue.
Today and always. Amen.

(*adapted from Carmina Gadelica*)

Lord, you brought me from the rest of last night to the joyous light of this day. Guide me from the new light of this day to the light of eternity. Amen.

(*unknown*)

Dear Lord Jesus, we shall have this day only once; before it is gone, help us to do all the good we can, so that today is not a wasted day.

(*Stephen Grellet*)

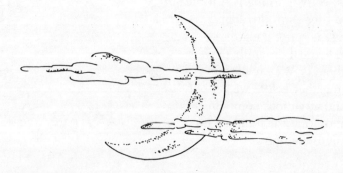

Bedtime prayers and blessings

I will lie down and sleep in peace, for you alone, O Lord, make me dwell in safety.

(*Ps. 4.8*)

Jesus, a look from you can embrace us with peaceful sleep, and ensure that our dreams are pure and holy. Bring peace, Lord, to our weary minds, and give rest to our tired limbs.

(*adapted from Ambrose of Milan*)

Guide us, O Lord, while waking,
and guard us while sleeping,
that awake we may watch with Christ,
and asleep we may rest in peace.

(*from Compline*)

Lighten our darkness, Lord, we pray; and in your mercy defend us from all perils and dangers of this night; for the love of your only Son, our Saviour Jesus Christ. Amen.

(*Gelasian Sacramentary*)

The Lord bless you and keep you; the Lord make his face to shine upon you and be gracious to you; the Lord lift up the light of his countenance upon you and give you his peace.

(*Num. 6.24–26*)

The Lord grant you a quiet night and a perfect rest. In the name of the Father, the Son and the Holy Spirit. Amen.

(*adapted from Compline*)

Silence is golden

Prayer is about communication. But communication does not always require words. Silence is an important but much neglected part of prayer.

Silence may also be a useful strategy for maintaining a family prayer time as children get older. Older children and teenagers may become self-conscious about praying aloud. Not infrequently they rebel against their parents' beliefs and feel resentment if they are forced to take part in something they are not sure they believe in.

We usually light a candle at about 10 p.m. and sit silently in the darkness for some time. At the end one of us will say the grace. Friends and visitors are always welcome to share this time with us. At present our children are too young to join in but we hope that as they grow older they will want to do so.

How long the period of silence will be depends very much on how familiar with silence the family is. Nowadays even many adults find more than four or five minutes hard to handle.

Praying around the cross

This is a form of silent prayer which originated in Eastern Europe but has been popularized by Taizé, an ecumenical community in France. On Friday evenings they place a large cross on the ground in the centre of their worship area. Participants simply kneel or lie around it, silently reflecting on what Christ has done for them. The reasoning behind this non-verbal form of prayer is that it signifies their desire to place their trust entirely in Christ. The cross is a graphic reminder of Christ's suffering on our behalf. An empty cross reminds us that, having triumphed over death, he is with us in the midst of our sufferings (small or large) whether or not we are aware of his presence.

If you have a simple wooden cross or a picture of the crucifixion, you might experiment with this as the focal point for a time of silent prayer.

A family prayer scrapbook

We have already mentioned the possibility of using prayer books in your family prayers. But why not create your own prayer book? All you need is a large scrapbook and the natural ingenuity of your children.

Include in the scrapbook whatever you find helpful. This may include prayers that you want to use regularly or memorize together, Bible readings, poems, pictures, photographs (perhaps of people for whom you pray regularly).

Letters to God

This idea was originally suggested to us by Morris West's novel *The Clowns of God*. In it a runaway pope uses open letters to God as a way of publicizing his views. We linked that with a technique of letter-writing, often used by secular journal keepers, to create an exercise for people who keep a prayer journal.[3]

Writing your prayers, perhaps in the form of a letter, can be a creative alternative to spoken prayers. These prayers might be collected in the family prayer scrapbook or, if they contain material that is too personal, they might be collected and burnt as part of your act of worship. The latter is particularly appropriate on occasions when the Christian year encourages us to focus on our sins and repentance.

~~~~~~

KEEPING SUNDAY SPECIAL

Every Sunday a celebration

Keeping Sunday special may suggest the wrong images. It is so easy to think of observing Sunday in terms of the things you shouldn't do. Lawrence can remember being present at a serious debate between several Christian students about whether it was all right to go hillwalking on Sunday. Was this rest or did the preparations amount to labour? Such legalism misses the point entirely.

Sunday is special not because it is shrouded in a cloud of regulations but because it is a day of celebration. In the calendar of the Church every Sunday is a feast day. Even during major fasts like Lent, Sundays are exempt (strictly speaking, the Sundays during Lent are not part of Lent at all).

This is because Sunday is the day of resurrection. It is the weekly celebration of Christ's victory over death and sin. As the first day of the new week, it points forward to the promise of a new creation. So it is the day when we celebrate hope in the face of death.

In other respects it resembles the old Jewish Sabbath. That was a day of rest; a day when people could escape from the enforced busyness of the secular world. Far from being a legalistic imposition it was a day of freedom from the drudgery of the everyday world.

An important aspect of family celebrations is the recapture of this sense of celebration every Sunday. Sundays should stand out from the rest of the week. In this way we begin to put some structure back into our experience of time (other than the structure imposed by work and school).

Time for church

For most Christians, Sunday is the day when they meet together to worship as the body of Christ. So what should be the relationship between our family prayers and the larger gatherings of the Church?

We would see them as complementary rather than in competition. One of our aims in family worship will be to help our children see the relevance and meaning of the larger gathering. We may do this in a variety of ways. One way is to make connections between what we do in the week and what is done in church, such as by using the same hymn or chorus books, by including in our daily prayers the same kinds of things as are to be found in church on Sunday, by following the same lectionary, etc.

If set prayers are in regular use in our public worship we might consider teaching them to our children and explaining their significance. For

example, we have gradually taught our children the basic elements of the
Rite A Communion Service from the Alternative Service Book. Long
before they could read, they knew when to declare 'Christ has died, Christ
is risen, Christ will come again'. Familiarity with the service is one way in
which we can encourage our children to take part. Of course, we also need
to explain the various parts of the service.

Afterwards it may be helpful to talk about what has happened. As
children get older this gives them an opportunity to think about and
perhaps disagree with the sermon in a secure context.

Church is more than a place or an act of worship. First and foremost it is
the people who take part. We say that we are all part of the same body.
Sunday is a particularly appropriate day for extending the hospitality of
our family to other parts of the body of Christ, inviting those who are on
their own to be part of our family celebrations. It is also a good day for
visiting old friends and acquaintances, maintaining and developing links
with Christians elsewhere.

Preparing for Sunday

In Jewish family traditions, preparations for the Sabbath are an important
part of the week. By contrast, there is relatively little emphasis within
Christianity on preparing for Sunday as a family. However, there are
community traditions of preparing for Sunday, and Anglican and
Catholic traditions of individual preparation for receiving communion
that we might draw on.

At Taizé they use a form of the Easter Eve Festival of Lights every
Saturday evening. We too might like to make the coming Sunday the
focal point of family prayers on Saturday evenings. If we belong to a
denomination with a liturgical tradition we might do this by drawing on
elements of the Sunday service; for instance, we might use the Collect for
the day and one of the readings set in the lectionary. Even if you cannot
draw upon such a tradition, it is probable that the Bible readings for the
following Sunday will be published in advance by your church. Why not
use them in your family prayers on Saturday?

2
Advent

THE MEANING OF ADVENT

Advent is traditionally a time of preparation. It was originally conceived as a six-week period of fasting and prayer in preparation for Christmas, modelled on the six-week period of Lent immediately preceding the other great Christian festival of Easter. However, over the centuries it was gradually shortened from six weeks to four.

During Advent, Christians prepare spiritually for the celebration of Christmas. But the season looks forward as well as back. As we anticipate Christmas, we also remember Christ's promise that he will come again. The waiting period of Advent reflects both the centuries before Christ's birth during which the Jewish people awaited the coming of their Messiah and our waiting for his return.

THE COUNTDOWN TO CHRISTMAS

Since Advent is a period of anticipation and preparation it is not surprising that Advent traditions focus particularly on marking the countdown to Christmas. Of course we all count the days to Christmas: our consumer society is only too eager to remind us that there are only X shopping days before Christmas. One sometimes gets the impression that the secular equivalent of Advent begins in October!

It comes as little surprise that every year church leaders exhort Christians to get back to the true spirit of Christmas. Surely there are more appropriate ways of celebrating the incarnation of our Lord than this spectacle of over-consumption we call Christmas.

We believe the traditional ways of marking the days until Christmas do allow us a different way of counting. And, perhaps because of the secular emphasis on material consumption, this different perspective is particularly important today. Looked at afresh, these traditions allow us time to reflect on the why and the who of Christmas. We may begin to re-examine the decorations and the drinks, the preparations and the presents. They also encourage us to examine ourselves; to seek out anything that may hinder the coming of the Lord in our own lives.

This emphasis on waiting is an excellent way of communicating the message of Advent to very young children. They may be too young to cope with an explanation of the historical origins of Advent, or to understand the longing of the Jews for the Messiah. But waiting for a special treat is something they can grasp. In this case we are waiting for a very special birthday party: Jesus' birthday party.

Advent wreaths

The old German tradition of making an Advent wreath is probably the most basic way of marking the weeks immediately before Christmas. It consists of a simple circle woven from twigs of evergreens with four candles (traditionally purple, though white candles with purple ribbons around them may be used instead) around its circumference. The wreath is completed by placing a fifth (white) candle in the centre to be lit on Christmas Day.

The wreath is a rich source of symbols which help to remind us of the significance of Advent. A circle is one of the traditional ways of symbolizing eternity since it has no beginning and no end. The living green of the twigs from which it is made contrast with the colourlessness and lifelessness of this time of year, reminding us of God's promise of new life for the lifeless fulfilled so completely in Christ's coming. The candles remind us of the light of Christ shining in the darkness of the world. Their number, four, represents the four weeks of Advent but, beyond that, they remind us of the centuries during which the faithful remnant of Israel waited for the coming of the Messiah and of the millenia during which Christians have awaited his second coming. The purple of the candles reminds us that it is a king for whom we wait. The increasing amount of light as more candles are lit each week announces that the celebration of Christ's coming draws steadily closer. Finally the fifth candle, for Christmas Day, is white and represents Christ the Light of the World.

Assembling the Advent wreath is an activity which could involve all the family in different ways: gathering the evergreens, weaving them together, you might even like to consider making your own candles (see 'Easter candles', p. 94). With parental supervision this is a safe and enjoyable activity for quite young children: our daughter made her first candle when she was four. Perhaps the Saturday before Advent Sunday would be a good day to have a go at making your own Advent wreath.

Dedication of the Advent wreath

When you have finished making the wreath you might like to hold a simple service to dedicate the wreath to its use as a reminder of the religious significance of Advent. Here is one possible pattern.

Leader: 'May this Advent wreath remind us of God's people patiently waiting for the Christ to come. May it remind us that Jesus was born to be God's light in the world, God-with-us. May it remind us to prepare our own hearts for Jesus to come afresh into them.'

All: 'O God, bless this wreath that, as we look at it, we may remember Jesus' coming and prepare our hearts for his coming again.'

Leader: 'As we light this candle, help us to keep our hearts lit by your love.'

(During this prayer another member of the family may light the first candle.)

Song: 'Come thou long-expected Jesus' (AMNS 31, MP 102)
            'Hark, the glad sound' (AMNS 30, JP 68, MP 210, SOF 154)
            'How lovely on the mountains' (JP 84, MP 249, SOF 192)
            'O come, O come, Emmanuel' (AMNS 26, JP 177, MP 493,
            SOF 410)

It is perfectly possible to begin such a tradition with very young children.
We have done this with our own children since they were toddlers.
However, as with all family prayer, you should allow for the fact that very
young children are unlikely to sit quietly through a long spoken act of
worship. In our family we pared the service down to the bare minimum
when the children were younger.

Another practical consideration is the location. In order to keep
younger children under control (and out of reach of the candles), you
might like to use your Advent wreath as a table decoration and light the
candle at the beginning of a family meal. Toddlers are securely strapped
into highchairs and the anticipation of food to come will keep older
children firmly anchored in place. If your family meal takes place in the

evening, the fact that it is dark by then underscores the symbolism of a light shining in the darkness.

With an older family it would be possible to place the wreath on a coffee table instead. It could become a focal point for family prayers every evening.

If you are worried about naked flames, a good alternative to the traditional Advent wreath is the Advent wreath banner illustrated on page 23. Instead of real candles, cloth ones may be attached to the appropriate parts of the banner by means of velcro.

Using the wreath in worship

You could use a similar pattern of dedication as you light the remaining candles each week during Advent. This might be done at the beginning of Sunday dinner or, if you maintain a pattern of preparation for Sunday worship, during evening prayers on Saturday.

Reading: Advent 1: Isa. 52.7–10; Rom. 13.9b–12; or Luke 21.25–33
               Advent 2: Isa. 55.1–5; or Mark 1.15
               Advent 3: Isa. 40.1–5; 1 Cor. 4.5; or John 1.19–28
               Advent 4: Isa. 11.1–5; or Luke 1.26–38a

Prayer: Week 1:   'Lord Jesus, Light of the World, you were born in a stable to be a king. Be born in our hearts as we wait for Christmas, be king of our lives today. Amen.'

               Week 2:   'Dear God, we thank you for the Bible and its promises of Jesus' coming. May its words fill our minds and our hearts with light. Amen.'

               Week 3:   'Lord Jesus, Light of the World, John the Baptist told the people to get ready for your coming. Help us to get ready as Christmas approaches. Amen.'

               Week 4:   'Dear God, you chose Mary to be Jesus' mother. Help us to follow her example of faith, joy and obedience now and always. Amen.'
                       (During this prayer, the appropriate number of candles may be lit.)

Hymn: one or more verses of a favourite Advent hymn

Remember that, though you may prefer variety, any young children present will derive more benefit from repetition. Choose one or two really well-known Bible verses appropriate to Advent (e.g. the opening sentences provided for each Sunday in Advent) and use them frequently throughout the season. Similarly choose your favourite Advent hymn and sing one or two verses again and again. The frequent repetition will enable your children to absorb important aspects of Advent quite effortlessly.

Advent calendars

A well-known alternative to the Advent wreath is the Advent calendar. This usually consists of a picture containing twenty-five windows (one for each day of December until Christmas). As each window is opened a scene appropriate to the season is revealed. In many families it is taditional to give each child an Advent calendar so that they can count down to Christmas by opening one window each day.

The principle is a good one. Unfortunately an increasing number of commercially available Advent calendars seem to treat Christmas in an entirely secular fashion. The scenes depicted are of the presents good children might receive (teddy bears, sweeties, etc.), of Christmas goodies (turkeys, trees, and crackers), of reindeer pulling sleighs, and of Santa Claus squeezing down chimneys! It is worth putting some effort into finding an Advent calendar that reflects the religious significance of the season rather than its commercialism.

Alternatively, you could encourage your children to make their own Advent calendars. These can be complicated or very simple efforts, depending on the age and dexterity of the children.

This year our eldest daughter made a simple Advent calendar for the weeks of Advent. The pictures for each week were cut from old Christmas cards. These were mounted on a large sheet of card in the shape of a house and hidden behind card windows. A nativity scene also culled from an old Christmas card was mounted behind the door of the house (to be opened on Christmas Day). As a final touch, she wrote the text 'He is coming soon' on the windows (one word on each window).

An older child might like to draw his or her own pictures for each of the windows. Another variation would be to draw the pictures on greaseproof paper using felt-tipped pens, cut holes in the card mount, and hang the whole thing in a window for a stained glass effect.

Other do-it-yourself possibilities include:

- *Advent jigsaw puzzle*: All this requires is an old Christmas card (preferably fairly large) with an appropriate picture. Mount it on stiff card (or, for a more permanent puzzle, on thin plywood) and cut it into twenty-five pieces. As you might expect, the puzzle can be assembled a piece at a time until, on Christmas day, it is completed to reveal a nativity scene. Perhaps an older child could make one for younger brothers or sisters.

- *The road to Bethlehem*: Draw a road with twenty-four paving stones in it, running from a picture of an eastern city to a nativity scene (both obtainable from Christmas cards). For each day in Advent a child can colour in one of the paving stones or (if the stones are big enough) paste on to it a picture from an old Christmas card.

- *Advent paper-chain*: This can be built up day by day, using strips of paper in seasonal colours. On Christmas Eve (perhaps after its maker has gone to bed), attach the ends of the paper-chain to a large picture of the nativity and hang it up as a Christmas decoration.

- *Advent candle*: This is simply a large candle calibrated from one to twenty-five down the side. The candle can be lit for each evening meal during Advent. If you can't find a suitable commercial candle, this might be a project for keen amateur candlemakers.

● *The Jesse tree*: This is yet another way of marking the passage of time in Advent. It begins with a bare branch. This can be mounted in a pot weighted with earth so that it can stand securely on a table.

During Advent read Old Testament stories relating to Jesus' genealogy. Talk about the stories and decide what symbols might remind people of those stories. Then ask the children to make the symbols. (For Anglican families this may be a particularly appropriate project for the second Sunday in Advent when their calendar concentrates on the word of God in the Old Testament.)

Some of the more common symbols include an apple (representing Adam and Eve); the ark (Noah); an altar (the story of Abraham and Isaac); the coat of many colours (Joseph); stone tablets (Moses and the giving of the law); a key and crown (King David); a scroll (the prophets); a shell and water (John the Baptist). They could be drawn on paper or card, built up from dough or modelling clay, cut out of cardboard, or made using any other construction techniques your children are familiar with.

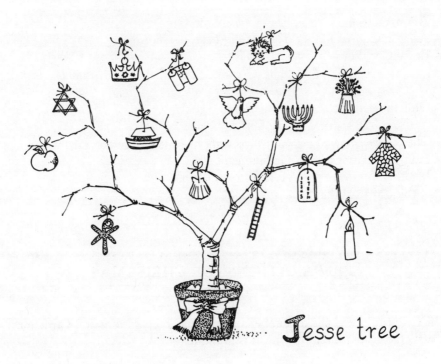

Jesse tree

When the symbols are complete they are placed upon the tree. As you get closer and closer to Christmas so the Jesse tree gradually fills up with symbols reminding the family of the history of preparation for the first coming of Jesus.

- *Advent mobile*: This is a simpler alternative for young children. It can be fashioned from an old wire coat-hanger. Each week the children could draw a picture representing the readings in church (or in the home). These are then hung from the coat-hanger by lengths of thread or wool.

Music for Advent and Christmas

J S Bach	*Christmas Oratorio*
Berlioz	*L'enfance du Christ*
Bliss	*A Prayer to the Infant Jesus*
Britten	*A Boy is Born*
	A Ceremony of Carols
Handel	*Messiah*
Messaien	*La Nativité du Seigneur*
Vaughan Williams	*Hodie*
Anonymous 4	*This Yoolis Night*
Atlanta Chorus	*The Many Moods of Christmas*
Bruce Cockburn	*Christmas*
	'The Cry of a Tiny Babe' from *Nothing But a Burning Light*
Graham Kendrick	*Rumours of Angels*
	The Gift
The King's Singers	*Christmas with the King's Singers*
Late Late Service	*God in the Flesh*
Maddy Prior and	*A Tapestry of Carols*
the Carnival Band	*Carols and Capers*

PREPARATIONS FOR CHRISTMAS

Obviously there are a number of practical preparations for Christmas which are appropriate to the season of Advent.

Cards and presents

Children may be encouraged to make their own Christmas cards or gift-wrap and, if there is time, home-made Christmas presents are always welcomed (especially by grandparents).

- *Potato printing*: One very simple way of mass-producing Christmas cards or gift-wrap is potato printing. All that is required is half a potato, its flat surface carved to form a suitable relief image (e.g. a star of Bethlehem), and a supply of paint. Simply apply the paint to the carved surface and apply the potato to a blank card or sheet of plain paper.

- *Pomanders*: These are very easy to make and are lovely little seasonal presents. You will need oranges (or firm apples), a good supply of cloves, and some brightly coloured ribbon. Stick the cloves firmly over the whole surface of the orange. Then wrap a piece of ribbon round it so that it can be hung up.

  For a more permanent present, you can preserve the pomander in the traditional fashion. After inserting the cloves, rub the surface of the orange with a mixture of equal parts ground cinnamon and powdered orris-root. This is most conveniently done with a small brush. Then wrap the pomander in greaseproof paper for a few weeks for the preservative to take effect.

  It is sometimes pointed out that their scent is a reminder of the spices which were part of the gifts brought to Jesus by the Magi. This would be a good family project in preparation for Epiphany. As you make the pomanders as gifts for family and friends you could talk together about the gifts of the wise men and their significance.

The Christmas tree

Christmas wouldn't be the same without a Christmas tree. Therefore it may come as a surprise to learn that they did not become popular in Britain until Victorian times. Prior to that the dressing of a Christmas tree was primarily a German custom. It owes its popularity in this country to Prince Albert. Even in Germany the custom is only a few hundred years old. Some say that Luther was the first person to have a Christmas tree in his home. However, it seems more likely to have originated later. We know that by the sixteenth century, German families were using evergreen branches decorated with apples, nuts, and sweets as Christmas decorations.

It is thought that the original inspiration for this custom came from the medieval mystery plays which were such an important form of Christian education for the illiterate masses. There was an Advent tradition of performing the 'Paradise Play', telling the story of the creation of man and woman, their disobedience, and the promise of salvation. The only scenery used was a fir-tree decorated with apples: the paradise tree.

But why are Christmas trees now decorated with lights? Apparently the practice of placing candles upon the tree evolved to underline the promise of salvation. Like the candles in the Advent wreath they symbolize Jesus Christ who is the Light of the World.

Decorations

In our family the dressing of the Christmas tree is usually kept until the last few days of Advent (between the last Sunday in Advent and Christmas Day itself). But earlier in Advent, the family could spend time together making Christmas decorations.

- *Popcorn garlands*: Thread pieces of popcorn together to make an edible alternative to paper-chains.

- *Baked tree decorations*: One year some Canadian friends of ours spent several happy hours with our eldest daughter, baking and painting Christmas tree decorations. These can be made from the following play-dough recipe:

> 8 oz (250 g) plain flour   2 tbsp (15 ml) cooking oil
> 4 oz (125 g) salt   water

Mix together the flour and salt. Add the oil and enough water to make a non-sticky dough. Knead the dough well.

When the dough is ready, roll it out into a sheet about ¼-inch thick and cut out a variety of festive shapes. Alternatively you could mould the dough into Christmas decorations.

Place the decorations on a foil-lined baking sheet and bake in the bottom of your oven at 180°C (Gas mark 4) for about 30 minutes. Allow them to cool and paint them.

• *Christmas crib*: We will say more about this when we deal with Christmas, but it is appropriate to mention it in passing here since making it is an Advent activity.

Nativity scenes can be made from almost anything. They can be plaited from straw, cut out of cardboard, constructed from balsa wood, pine-cones, pebbles from the beach. Dolls can be dressed up in appropriate costumes to act the parts. One year our daughter made an entire nativity scene (Mary, Joseph, baby Jesus, manger, donkey, sheep, shepherds, angels, and three kings) from the cardboard cores of toilet rolls! It took equal place alongside our professionally-made nativity scene (one which we find evocative since it was made in Bethlehem by Arab Christians using local olive wood).

- *Christmas mural*: For this, you will need a large sheet of card or brown wrapping paper, glue, and a supply of decorative wrapping paper (save the gift-wrap from your presents). Everyone can join in. Each person chooses some paper and cuts out stars, suns, candles, hearts (whatever expresses the joy of Christmas). The resultant shapes can be pasted on to the large sheet and the whole thing hung up to remind us of the joy that Jesus has brought.

  Another possibility would be to use the mural to re-tell the Christmas story. If you lack the artistic skills to draw figures, etc., you could use old Christmas cards.

- *Pine-cone trees*: These are easy to make from large pine-cones and plastic drinking cups (or empty yoghurt pots). Trim the cup (or pot) to a little less than half the height of the pine-cone. Cover it with paper and decorate with felt-tipped pens, bands of coloured paper, sequins or tinsel. Alternatively cover it in coloured foil or Christmas wrapping paper.

  Decorate the cone with glitter powder. One way of fixing the cone to its pot is by mixing up some polyfilla, filling the pot with it and inserting the cone 'tree' before the mixture has set. Another possibility would be to fill the pot with plasticine.

- *Christmas bells*: You can make these by cutting out the sections of plastic egg cartons and spraying them with silver or gold spray paint. The clapper is made by piercing the top of the bell, threading through a length of decorative yarn and tying on a foil-covered bead. They can be hung together in clusters to create an attractive Christmas tree decoration.

- *Christmas banner*: Why not make a banner to celebrate Christ's coming into the world? The one illustrated on page 23 has removable candles held in place by velcro and could be used as an alternative to the Advent wreath.

Cooking

Christmas would not be complete without celebratory meals and special foods. The preparation of some of these is an integral part of Advent.

- *Christmas pudding*: Traditionally, this is made on or about the Sunday before Advent, which is called 'Stir-Up Sunday' because of the Collect for this in the Church of England's Book of Common Prayer:

  'Stir up, we beseech thee, O Lord, the wills of thy faithful people;

that they, plenteously bringing forth the fruit of good works, may of thee be plenteously rewarded; through Jesus Christ our Lord. Amen.'

- *Christmas cake*: Another traditional part of Christmas celebrations is the Christmas cake. Icing and decorating the cake is an activity which can involve the children during Advent. We got fed up with Christmas cakes covered in snowmen, penguins, and Father Christmases. Instead we decided to cover our cake with decorations reminding us of the true significance of Christmas. Using a block of marzipan and food colouring, our four-year-old daughter was able to make a baby lying in a manger. Perhaps in future years we will extend the idea to create an entire nativity scene on the cake.

OTHER ADVENT IDEAS

Advent suggestion box

This is an idea for a very different kind of Advent preparation. As we await the coming of Christ our preparations should be inward as well as outward. The suggestion box is a tangible reminder of that inward preparation.

At the beginning of Advent a box is decorated and filled with cards containing suggestions. The whole family can take part in making the box, with children decorating it and parents writing out the cards (making sure that suggestions by the children themselves are well represented). These will typically be 'good deeds' that the recipient of the card might perform. For example, a card might ask you to read to your little sister, or

write a letter to Granny, or help with the washing up, or a busy parent
might be asked to spend extra time with the children. In families where
there is a wide range of ages it might be a good idea to colour code the
cards so that suggestions for each age group are on a single colour.

Weekly (or more frequently) members of the family pick a card from the
box after a meal. Sometime during that day (or week) they must carry out
the suggestion on the card. Try not to make the suggestions unpleasant
chores – children are more likely to view Advent positively if the
associated traditions are fun!

Advent collection box

Alternatively, you might put an Advent collection box on the meal table.
This need be nothing more elaborate than a cardboard box with a slit cut
in the top. The children might be encouraged to decorate it in a seasonal
fashion or cover it in pictures representing the charity to which the money
will be going. Make one meal each day a simple affair (e.g. bread and soup
for lunch) and put the money saved in the collection box. Individual
family members might be encouraged to cut down on sweets and other
luxuries during this period and add what they save to the collection. This
idea could be adapted for younger children who do not yet have money of
their own by making available a supply of coins (brand new 2p or 5p
pieces). As a special reward for being good they might be allowed to put
one of these coins in the collection box. During Christmas (perhaps on
Boxing Day) the money saved can be donated to a suitable charity.

Advent prayer wheel

One idea which we have tried with our children is to make an Advent
prayer wheel. This consists of a large circle of card divided into four equal
segments by lines running through the centre. Around the circumference
of each segment we write the prayer theme for each week of Advent.
These can be agreed upon in advance by members of the family.

Each week we turn the relevant segment to the top as a reminder of the
people or issues we have agreed to pray about that week. Family members
are encouraged to fill up the segments with short written prayers, pictures,
photographs, or anything else which is relevant to that prayer theme.

A *waiting book*

This is the Advent equivalent of a Lenten journal. In it we collect anything which reminds us of the Advent theme of waiting. These may be pictures, stories, poems, or memories of anything we have had to wait for.

Planting a bulb

Waiting for a bulb to flower is a good way of conveying to children the experience of waiting which is at the heart of Advent. Hyacinths are a popular choice. Other possibilities might include narcissi, snowdrops and crocuses. Or there is always the spectacular hippeastrum (amaryllis).

Narcissus or hyacinth bulbs may be planted at the beginning of Advent. They should be kept in darkness for about three weeks. At the beginning of the fourth week you may move them to a dimly lit spot. Keep them out of direct sunlight until the tops have turned bright green.

With luck, Christmas Day will be brightened by a hyacinth in flower!

Outdoor activities

Since the coming of light to overcome the darkness is a key symbol of
Advent and Christmas, walks which involve this theme are particularly
appropriate at this time of year. Taking the children out for a walk by
starlight is one possibility, pointing out the constellations to them and
reminding them that Jesus Christ is God's light in the darkness. Perhaps
you could read Gerard Manley Hopkins' lovely poem 'The Starlight
Night' to them.

This may not be possible for town- or city-dwellers because the
brightness of street lights swamps the starlight. Instead you could get the
family up early one morning to watch the sunrise. In this case Christ's
light dispelling the darkness is the theme to emphasize.

SPECIAL OCCASIONS IN ADVENT

Saints' days?

In addition to the great festivals celebrating the chief events of the gospel,
the Christian year is punctuated by a host of saints' days. Many Christians
take this pattern for granted. Others find the celebration of particular
saints rather offensive. For them it smacks of superstition and they fear it
may detract from the centrality of Jesus Christ.

What justification can be offered for remembering the lives and works
of particular Christians? The saints celebrated by the churches are
examples to us, not of outstanding holiness which we are called upon to
emulate by our own efforts, but of ordinary men and women whose lives
were transformed by the power of the Holy Spirit. When we celebrate
them, we recall not their efforts but the work of God through them and,
hence, God's capacity to work in our lives today.

Celebrating the lives of particular saints also serves to remind us that we
are not alone. They are individual members of that great cloud of
witnesses spoken of in Hebrews. Saints' days are a reminder that the
Church extends beyond what we can see here and now to embrace all
Christians in all times and all places.

But, if this is so, is the celebration of particular saints not rather élitist?
Looking at the very rigorous criteria for sainthood imposed by the Roman
Catholic Church one suspects that this may be the case. Other traditions

take a more flexible approach. For example, the Anglican calendar also includes many men and women who, though not officially saints, have made important contributions to the life of the Church. They include evangelical and Anglo-Catholic pioneers such as Charles Simeon, William Wilberforce, John Keble and Edward King. They include missionaries, social reformers and modern martyrs (such as Dietrich Bonhoeffer and Janani Luwum).

What about the doubtful historicity of some of the older saints? There is a sense in which this does not matter a great deal. Some, at least, of the traditional saints are significant not in their own right but because they have become symbols of particular Christian virtues. Thus, St Nicholas personifies generosity and St Valentine, Christian love. Celebrations of these saints become a concrete way of thinking about the virtue in question.

We may create our own personal calendar of saints: men and women who personify for us the Christian life. These may be official saints, unofficial Christian heroes or heroines. They may even be personal acquaintances.

St Nicholas' Day (6th December)

The feast day of St Nicholas is neglected in British traditions. He has been submerged in the secular tradition of Father Christmas to give us the corpulent red-clad figure of Santa Claus, flying through the winter skies with his reindeer, proving to good little girls and boys that being good brings material rewards.

We suspect that many Christian parents are a little uneasy about this tradition. It is very difficult to isolate our children from it. Even if we pretend it doesn't exist, they will hear about it at school or on the television. But what should we do? Do we go along with the myth of Father Christmas, pretending that Christmas presents come from him? Do we try to debunk the myth? And, if so, how do we avoid appearing to be kill-joys?

The Feast of St Nicholas seems to us to offer a positive way out of the dilemma. This early Christian martyr is, of course, the inspiration for the American form of Father Christmas: Santa Claus. Little is known of his life apart from the fact that he was Bishop of Myra. But the legends which have grown up around him seem particularly appropriate for this season of the year. Their common theme is his generosity. Here was someone who embodied the scriptural injunction 'Freely you have received, freely give' (Matt. 10.8).

● *The story of St Nicholas*

Nicholas was a rich man but his wealth did not make him happy.
He knew that many people living in the same town were very
poor. Nicholas was a Christian and knew that one way of
worshipping God was serving others. Perhaps he remembered that
Jesus had told the disciples, 'Whatever you did for one of the least
of these brothers of mine, you did for me' (Matt. 25.40).

Anyway he decided to share his money with the poor people of
the town. But he remembered another saying of Jesus: 'When you
give to the needy, do not let your left hand know what your right
hand is doing, so that your giving may be in secret. Then your
Father, who sees what is done in secret, will reward you' (Matt.
6.3–4). What was he to do? Poor Nicholas was so well known that
he couldn't possibly keep his good deeds secret.

One evening some time later he was walking home through the
town. It was a cold winter's night, probably near Christmas, and
snow was thick on the ground. As he passed one house he heard a
child crying. He stopped and listened. Then he heard another
child saying, 'Father, we are cold and hungry. Can't we go out into
the streets to beg?'

'No,' the father replied. 'You are too young and it is very cold
outside. We must pray and trust that God will help us.'

Hearing this, Nicholas realized that God wanted him to answer
this poor man's prayers. He hurried home through the snow, went
to the room where he kept his money, and filled three bags full of
gold coins. Then he trudged back through the snow to the poor
man's house. But how could he keep the man from realizing who
he was?

In those days the houses of poor people did not have proper
chimneys, just a hole in the wall to let the smoke out. Nicholas
saw that there was no smoke coming from their house. They were
obviously too poor to have a fire. All was quiet. The family must
be asleep. So Nicholas carefully reached up and dropped the three
bags of gold through the hole in the wall. Imagine the father's
surprise when he woke up the next morning to find all that money
just lying on the floor!

But, if he kept his giving so secret, how do we know that
Nicholas did this? Well, from then on, he would often go out at
night and bring gifts to poor families. From time to time people
would see him doing this and, although he asked them to keep it a
secret, some of them told their friends. And so the story spread.

You might find that some of the legends surrounding St Nicholas are suitable for telling to children on this day. The above is a version of the best known of these (and the one which gave rise to the symbol for St Nicholas, three bags of gold).

In our family we tell the story of St Nicholas at evening prayers on 5th December, St Nicholas' Eve. You might like to illustrate the story in some way. Perhaps you could get a postcard of an icon of St Nicholas (who is also patron saint of Russia). The children leave their slippers outside their bedroom doors and in the morning they wake up to find that three bags of gold (chocolate money) have appeared in them.

The great thing about this festival is its emphasis on generous giving rather than on receiving. Perhaps you could take some time on St Nicholas' Day to finalize your Christmas present list, or dispatch your presents, or have a family conference on which charity you are going to support this Christmas.

Another possibility is to encourage members of the family to be little St Nicholases. Issue a challenge to the family to do secret acts of kindness to one another that day.

• *St Nicholas biscuits*: A traditional activity for this day is the making of St Nicholas biscuits. These are ginger biscuits (any recipe will do) made in the shape of bishops. Older children can help weigh out the ingredients and prepare the dough (or this could be made while they are at school and kept in the fridge). Everyone can lend a hand when it comes to cutting out the shapes. Even our two-year-olds joined in (bishops were too hard for them but they managed to cut out star shapes which were stored for serving up on Christmas Day and at Epiphany).

3
Christmas and Epiphany

SOME CHRISTMAS TRADITIONS

Nativity scene

The reconstruction of the nativity scene has been a popular Christian custom for nearly eight centuries. Unlike the Christmas tree we can identify the originator of the tradition, which began in 1224 when St Francis of Assisi built a manger and conducted the first nativity play.

Suggestions for making your own nativity scene can be found in the chapter on Advent. It can be very simple or very elaborate but either way it is a strong visual reminder of the true significance of Christmas.

Christmas food

Like many traditional festivals, Christmas has its own distinctive traditional foods and drinks.

- *Mince pies*: Christmas just wouldn't be the same without mince pies. They can be purchased from the local baker or supermarket but somehow the ones you make yourself seem so much nicer.

  According to one tradition mince pieces should be round to represent the manger at Bethlehem (the mincemeat is the sweetness of the baby Jesus). The dimpled edges are the hills and valleys through which Joseph and Mary had to travel on their way to Bethlehem.

- *Mulled wine*: This is a traditional, and quite delicious, accompaniment to mince pies. It can be made with very inexpensive red wine (Lawrence is fond of winemaking and this recipe is a good way of using his failures).

  You will need: 1 pint (600 ml) water
  4 oz (125 g) caster sugar
  6 cloves
  $\frac{1}{4}$ tsp (1 ml) nutmeg (freshly grated, if possible)
  1 pinch cinnamon

  Mix the above in a large saucepan and boil for fifteen minutes.
  Then add: 2 slices of lemon
  the rind of half a lemon (grated)
  2 (0.75 l) bottles of red wine

  Alternatively, mix *all* the ingredients in a slow cooker and leave to warm up for a couple of hours.

  By the time the mulled wine is ready to serve it has been diluted by water and a good deal of alcohol will have evaporated away. Consequently some people add a little brandy to fortify it.

  On the other hand you may want a teetotal alternative. Why not try mulling an alchohol-free wine?

- *Spiced blackberry cordial*: We sometimes offer this as a non-alcoholic alternative to mulled wine. To make the concentrate, you need a quantity of blackberries (fresh or frozen). Rub the blackberries through a fine sieve (or pulp them in a food processor) and measure the amount of juice produced. For each pint of juice you need:

1 lb (450 g) sugar   8 cloves
    or 6 tbsp (90 ml) honey   1 tsp (5 ml) cinnamon

Put all the ingredients into a pan and bring the mixture slowly to the boil, stirring until the sugar has melted. Boil gently for 5 minutes. When it is cold the mixture can be bottled and stored in the fridge.

To serve, put 2 or 3 tablespoons of the concentrate into a mug and top up with boiling water.

● *Christmas bread*: Since Bethlehem means 'house of bread' it is appropriate to pay particular attention to the bread served up during Christmas.

Julekake (Norwegian Christmas bread):
       1 sachet dried yeast
       1 tsp sugar
       4 fl oz half milk/half water
       1 lb (450 g) plain flour
       1 egg
       1 tsp (5 ml) salt
       4 oz (125 g) butter
       4 oz (125 g) sugar
       1 tsp ground cardamom
       4 oz (125 g) raisins
       4 oz (125 g) mixed candied fruit
       4 oz (125 g) chopped almonds

Warm the milk/water mixture until hand hot. Whisk in the sugar followed by the yeast and leave in a warm place for about 15 minutes.

Sift the flour and salt into a mixing bowl. Add the sugar and rub in the butter to achieve a breadcrumb texture. Add the ground cardamom and stir in the egg. Finally, mix in the yeast liquid to create a dough.

Knead the dough and leave it in a warm place to rise to double its original size (about an hour and a half).

Knock back the dough and gradually add the raisins, nuts and candied fruit. Pat into a round loaf and place on a greased baking sheet. Cover with an oiled plastic bag and leave to rise for about half an hour. Remove the bag and bake in a pre-heated oven (190°C/Gas mark 5) for 45 minutes.

When the loaf is cool, decorate with white glacé icing and glacé cherries.

You might like to offer special rolls or croissants for breakfast on Christmas day rather than the usual toast.

Think about the ingredients that make up your celebratory loaf. Dates and figs have a particular association with Israel, the land of Jesus' birth. For Epiphany, it is traditional to choose spicy bread, the spices recalling the gifts of the Magi.

Making bread could be a special project to involve younger members of the family during the holiday season. The very fact that they have helped to make it will make even a very simple loaf seem quite special.

Christmas plants and flowers

There is a surprising range of flowering (or fruiting) plants which you may use to decorate your home in preparation for Christmas. In addition to the traditional choices of holly, ivy and mistletoe, you may be able to get hold of cotoneaster, winter flowering jasmine or mahonia. If you prefer living plants, poinsettias, African violets, kalanchoes and cyclamens are all very popular and easily available at this time of year.

Why not make a living centrepiece for your Christmas dinner table by putting some suitable pot plants in a wicker basket? Simply line the basket with plastic, insert the pots and surround them with sphagnum moss (to keep them in place and to keep the plants moist). Plants such as variegated ivy, kalanchoe, solanum and poinsettias would be suitable. Sprigs of holly or fir can be inserted into the moss to hide the pots and provide a background.

Hospitality and Christmas parties

Christmas is a traditional time of the year for parties. For much of the year we are simply too busy with work, meetings and so on that it is difficult to find time for deepening friendships and making new friends. The Christmas season offers us the perfect opportunity to slow down or (if possible) stop work altogether and devote ourselves to fun and fellowship.

Parties need not be elaborate. Here are some themes that you might like to try yourselves.

• *'Thank you' parties*: During Christmas we give thanks for the greatest gift in human history: God's gift of his own son. We celebrate the gift of his friendship. Why not invite those people we want to thank for being our friends and neighbours through the preceding year? We try to run a series of such parties: offering mince pies (or shortbread after the New Year) and mulled wine (or fruit juice for the children). The catering is simple and by choosing appropriate times they can be kept relatively effortless.

Don't forget your children's friends! This is a good time of year to instil the habit of saying thank you in our children. Seeing us do it is good, but giving them the opportunity as well is better still.

- *Pot-luck dinners*: Invite a few friends to come over one evening. Ask each to bring a dish and a story. For example, you could ask everyone to describe the Christmas that has meant most to them. Or, if that seems too personal, ask them to bring stories, anecdotes or poems with a Christmas connection.

- *Christmas carol parties*: If you are at all musical, get people together for a brief rehearsal and then go out carol singing together. Warm drinks and mince pies taste even better when you return from carol singing.

- *Games parties*: Ask people to bring a game. Traditional party games such as charades are fun, or alternatively, you could divide into teams and play a game like Trivial Pursuit.

- *Television party*: Television can be one of the greatest antisocial forces at Christmas or any other time of the year. Why not combat that tendency by inviting people to watch one of the better Christmas broadcasts together? If nothing appeals to you, try a suitable video. As for catering, it couldn't be simpler: large quantities of coke and popcorn (an American acquaintance of ours makes carrier bags full of popcorn for such occasions!).

Hospitality really comes into its own for couples without children or whose children have grown up and left home. If the preparations for Christmas seem too much for just the two of you, why not invite single members of your local church or overseas students to join you for Christmas? Having guests with whom to share the festivities gives fresh impetus to your celebrations. As Joanna Bogle points out: 'A guest at the Christmas table is what turns the feast into a real celebration, an excuse for the special decorations, Christmasy napkins, candles, crackers, toasts over the liqueurs.'[1]

THE TWELVE DAYS OF CHRISTMAS

Commercial pressures seem to have concentrated all our attention on a single day: Christmas Day itself. But in earlier Christian traditions it was a festival lasting the twelve days from Christmas to Epiphany. A vestige of this older tradition may be found in the carol, 'The Twelve Days of Christmas'.

We believe there are real advantages in spreading Christmas over twelve days. If the thought of repeating Christmas twelve times in a row seems too horrible to contemplate, you will appreciate the first of those advantages. You may be suffering from the way Christmas Day is hyped up. There is tremendous pressure for Christmas Day to be the perfect celebration ('of what?', one may ask). Over the past few years in the parish ministry, Diana has become increasingly conscious of the very great stress caused by the commercialism and the social expectations surrounding Christmas. Many people do approach it with dread and, as a result, the weeks before Christmas seem a popular time for marriages to break up.

People in that situation have actually said to us, 'I couldn't face another Christmas with . . .'

In our family we deliberately spread the Christmas festivities over twelve days to reduce the emphasis (and, therefore, pressure) on the first day of the festival. Instead of one enormous celebration with everyone opening and discarding all their presents, overeating and overdrinking, and getting irritated by all the guests, we have twelve mini-celebrations. Christmas presents are spread out over the twelve days, which has the added advantage that it gives children something new to occupy them every day of the school holidays.

A *nativity banner*

It is possible to make a Christmas banner to mark the twelve days of Christmas in the same way as an Advent calendar. If you use the simple banner-making technique described in Chapter 1, simply cut out a felt image each day and stick it on your banner. In this way you will gradually build up your own nativity scene. One possible order in which do to this might be:

1st day	manger
2nd day	Jesus (in manger)
3rd day	Mary
4th day	Joseph
5th day	stable
6th day	star
7th day	donkey
8th day	cow
9th day	shepherd
10th day	sheep
11th day	wise men
12th day	gifts of wise men

Alternatively you might prefer to make a simpler banner such as the one illustrated.

Christmas Eve

Our family act of worship for Christmas Eve is built around a Mexican custom known as *the Posada*. In its original form, this is a play in which the entire community participates during the days leading up to Christmas. The statues of Mary and Joseph are removed from the Church and carried in procession to one of the homes in the village. Next day the procession moves on to another household. In this way every family plays host to the statues for one night until they are returned to the Church on Christmas Eve.

We have modified this custom to create a kind of family nativity play. Since they were toddlers, our twins have played the parts of Mary and Joseph (dressed for their parts with the help of a couple of tea-towels and old ties!). By tradition, their older sister, Angela, is the angel. Di acts as the narrator. With the twins carrying figures of Mary and Joseph (taken from our nativity set), they form a little procession in order and march downstairs to the living room door, singing 'Little Donkey'. There they are confronted by Lawrence, the innkeeper, with a brusque 'Where do you think you're going? There's no room here for the likes of you.' And then in response to their entreaties, 'Oh, very well. You can find a place in the stable.' Lawrence then leads the procession to the nativity scene and the twins put the figures of Mary and Joseph in their proper places. This is followed by a very brief service.

> *Leader*: 'God of love, bless this manger. May it remind us of the birth of your Son, Jesus Christ, and may the light of his goodness shine upon us all.'
>
> *All*:   first verse of 'Away in a manger'
>
> Procession to dinner table
>
> Lighting of Advent wreath
>
> *All*:   fourth verse of 'O little town of Bethlehem'

Christmas Day

We may succeed in keeping Advent Christ-centred rather than consumption-centred and then lose the battle on Christmas Day itself. It is only too easy for the presents, party food, and television programmes to supplant the incarnation as the real meaning of Christmas. We have already mentioned our practice of spreading the giving of gifts over the twelve days as one way of reducing the emphasis on presents. But we need to do more if we are to redeem this festival from the clutches of western materialism.

One way to establish a Christ-centred atmosphere is to play appropriate seasonal music. Christmas hymns, religious carols, or extracts from the riches of classical music can all help to create an apropriate atmosphere. If you have suitable equipment, you might like to use something like 'For unto us a child is born' from Handel's Messiah to awaken the household. Perhaps everyone could dance down to breakfast?

By all means let the family watch television. But on this day, of all days, it should be carefully monitored! If you possess a video recorder it is a relatively easy matter to plan and control what appears in your living-room.

What about family worship on Christmas Day? As with Sundays, we assume that most Christian families will want to meet other Christians on this day to celebrate the incarnation of our Lord. Therefore, any family act of worship is best kept fairly simple.

One idea which may help to remind children of the real significance of Christmas is that of the incarnation as God's gift to us. All the presents we give and receive at Christmas pale into insignificance when compared with this, the greatest of all gifts.

● *Christmas dinner*: This is no ordinary dinner. We treat Christmas dinner as a birthday meal. After all, we are celebrating Jesus' birthday. All the usual festive preparations are an important part of the day. Every member of the family can lend a hand: younger children may be commissioned to make festive covers for your usual place mats, perhaps drawing or painting Christmas scenes, or using the wrapping paper from opened presents to make a collage.

The menu is a matter of individual taste. However, one suggestion which you may like to consider is to keep the dessert fairly light. Childhood memories of conspicuous overeating followed by older family members snoring in front of the television have made us reluctant to serve up the full traditional Christmas dinner at one sitting. We prefer to have the turkey with all the trimmings followed by some special fruit at lunch-time, while the Christmas pudding is reserved for supper-time.

The Christmas cake is not forgotten. We tend to make this an afternoon event and we sing 'Happy Birthday' to Jesus as we cut the cake. You may prefer some other time. Different families have very different traditions – we have even heard of families who eat their Christmas cake at breakfast! This may reflect the Norwegian tradition of eating the *Julekake* described above for breakfast on Christmas Day.

• *The Christmas grace:*

Leader: We give you thanks for the wonder of birth and, in particular, for the birth of your Son, Jesus Christ, who came to bring us light.

Lighting of Advent wreath and central candle (perhaps by an older child)

All: Chorus of 'O come all ye faithful'

Leader: We give you thanks, O God, for the food and drink before us. As we celebrate together may we remember the One whose birthday this is.

All: *Raise glasses and wish one another 'Merry Christmas'.*

St Stephen's Day (26th December)

The day after Christmas is traditionally the festival of St Stephen, the first Christian martyr. We are told in Acts that he was one of those appointed by the apostles to be a deacon. In other words, it was his particular ministry to look after the needy.

Probably because of this connection with giving, it became traditional for those who could to give presents to the less well off on this day. Masters gave presents to their servants; the churches opened their poor boxes and distributed the contents (hence, its popular name, Boxing Day); and, to this day, people give Christmas boxes to paper boys, postmen, milkmen, etc.

This is a particularly appropriate day on which to make decisions about one's giving, or to distribute any money you saved for charity during Advent. Again this is something which children may be encouraged to take a part in.

A good carol to use in family worship today would be 'Good King Wenceslas'. The events described in the song are supposed to have occurred on this day, and they reflect the theme of giving to the needy. The most appropriate biblical reading would, of course, be an abbreviated version of the story of St Stephen (Acts 6.8—7.2a, 7.51–60).

St John's Day (27th December)

This is the day on which the Church has traditionally remembered the life and ministry of St John the Evangelist. Since two of the chief features of his writings are his emphasis on light and on love these are particularly appropriate themes for the day's activities and worship. One or two of the Advent activities emphasizing light might be tried today (such as getting everyone up to watch the sunrise or a candle-making session).

Worship will follow the usual pattern. Appropriate verses to read would include John 1.1–5, 14, or 1 John 2.10. And you might like to sing choruses such as 'The light of Christ' (*Fresh Sounds* 98) or 'In the stillness of the night' (MP 526, *Sound of Living Waters* 2).

Holy Innocents (28th December)

The brutal murder of the children of Bethlehem on Herod's orders (Matt. 2.13–18) seems out of place in a season of celebration. But it is probably precisely because of its jarring note that it has become traditional to recall the massacre during the Christmas season (true chronology would seem to suggest a date after Epiphany). It reminds us that Christmas cannot be divorced from Good Friday; that we are celebrating the birth of a child into a world broken by sin, a child who would himself be broken for the sake of our sin.

In some parts of Britain it has been (not surprisingly) a day of mourning. A more positive tradition is to make the day child-centred. Since we have three young children, we stress the latter. It is a day for the children to have their friends to a party. As with the whole of Christmas the secret of retaining your sanity is to keep it simple. Enlist your children to help in the preparations; use the biscuits and other party food they helped make during Advent.

During family prayers put particular emphasis on children. Think about and pray for children in other lands (perhaps scenes from the television can prompt you). In our prayers we remember in particular a group of children in a very poor part of Lima where a family friend works as a missionary.

New Year's Eve

It may come as a surprise to some readers to realize that the celebration of the new year in the middle of winter is a relatively recent innovation. Until the change from the older Julian calendar to the Gregorian calendar, the new year was celebrated in early April. By moving the new year to the middle of winter it became associated with the pagan festival of Yule. Some Christians are suspicious of these pagan connections. However, this celebration can be given a positive Christian dimension.

It is traditionally a time for recalling the old and preparing for the new. In any culture which is conscious of its own past it is a natural time for celebrating the glories of that culture. Nowhere is this more true than in Scotland where Hogmanay was until relatively recently a more important festival than Christmas.

Lawrence was brought up in Scotland and, although he has not lived there for some years, finds it perfectly natural to celebrate his Scottish heritage on New Year's Eve. Old records are dug out of little-used record cases and Scottish folk-songs fill the night air. And should anyone of Scottish origin be spending the New Year with us the conversation will be dominated by tales of Scotland. Last year, for example, talk turned to the Highland clearances.

But even if you have no such sense of personal involvement in your cultural history, New Year may still be a valuable time for examining your roots in the recent as well as the more distant past. It is a time for digging out the old family photograph albums and recalling the joys and sorrows of past years. Perhaps each family member could be asked to select one photograph from the past year. Ask them to choose one which represents that for which they have most cause to give thanks. Share those photographs during family prayers that day; use them as a basis for giving thanks to God for the past year.

Another possibility is to keep a family journal. New Year's Eve is an appropriate time for the official journal-keeper of the family (or each member) to write a summary of the past year.

But New Year is a time for looking forward as well as looking back. If we look back at the losses, sorrows, endings, and failures of the old year, we do so in order to make room for the possibilities, promises, and hopes of the new. We can consciously put behind us those missed opportunities, anxieties and regrets. When we have shed them, we can look forward hopefully to a new day, a new year and new opportunities.

Having reviewed the old year and given thanks for our experiences, we should ask ourselves what we shall be taking with us into the New Year. The practice of making New Year's resolutions tends to be sneered at. Such commitments are notoriously short-lived. But the transition from one year to another is a good time to consider what changes you would like to see in your own life and that of your family. Perhaps you could discuss your lifestyle together as a family and make communal decisions about areas in which you would like to see changes. These could then be integrated into a brief family act of rededication to God's service on New Year's Day.

New Year's Day

In the Anglican calendar this day is kept as the Naming of Jesus. It is, in fact, the eighth day after Christmas: the day on which a baby boy would be circumcised and named in Jewish tradition. This day is a day of new beginnings. The theme of new beginnings can be emphasized by reading part of the creation story from Genesis 1 and 2.

Naming had much greater significance for the Jews than it does for us. Look again at Genesis 1: it was as God named the various parts of creation that they took shape. The name reflected the character of its owner or vice versa. The name Jesus means 'Yahweh is salvation', and his other names and titles also point to the work he was to accomplish.

It might be interesting to get hold of a dictionary of names and find out what the names of your family and friends mean. Some people stress the importance of names by serving cakes with individual names done in icing (or initials formed from sweets).

Here is one possible pattern for a family service of rededication.

Leader:	'Behold I make all things new; I am Alpha and Omega, the Beginning and the End.'
Song:	'Jesus, name above all names' (MP 375, SOF 298)
Reading:	*an appropriate passage for this day would be the story of the presentation of Jesus in the Temple (Luke 2.15–21; or just v. 21 if the family is young).*
Sharing:	*of the family's agreed New Year resolution*
Leader:	'Lord, we give you thanks for bringing us safely to the beginning of another year: Forgive us the wrongs we have done in the past year, and help us to forgive the wrongs done to us that we might grow in our relationships and glorify you.

As we look forward to the year ahead
Give us the faith to see you with us;
the hope to keep pressing onwards;
the love which is above all things;
and the courage to begin again whenever we falter.'

Thank You Card Day

This is an idea we have adapted from a suggestion by the American
liturgist Joan Halmo. It appealed to us because of our childhood memories
of being forced to write interminable 'thank you' letters during the
Christmas holidays. Forcing a child to sit with a pen and blank piece of
paper day after day is a recipe for frayed nerves!

Learning to express gratitude for what others have done for us is an
important experience for adults and children alike. It ought not to be
turned into a chore. The whole point of Halmo's Thank You Card Day is
to transform the writing of 'thank you' letters into an enjoyable family
project.

Making suitable cards is simple. The potato stamp method described in
the last chapter is very effective. Alternatively you can cut out suitable
pictures from the Christmas cards you have received and mount them on
card. Last year our children traced and cut out card outlines of steam
engines. The message need be no more than a simple 'thank you' and the
child's signature (or mark). It is certainly not necessary to make children
write entire essays to obscure relations.

The timing of Thank You Card Day will depend largely on your strategy
for opening Christmas presents. If most or all presents are opened on
Christmas Day itself it is probably best to encourage the family to respond
before New Year. December 29th and 30th are good days since there are
no major traditional festivals or celebrations on those days. If, like us, you
spread the opening of presents over the twelve days of Christmas then a
date closer to Epiphany is more suitable. By contriving the distribution of
presents so that those opened after Thank You Card Days are from
immediate family members you can get around any need for a second bout
of letter writing.

Epiphany (6th January)

This is the day on which western churches celebrate the coming of the
Magi to worship the infant Jesus. In our home, today is the day when we
finally install the Magi in our nativity scene. Until this time they will

gradually have been moving from shelf to shelf across the room, each day getting a little closer to their destination.

- *An Epiphany party*: This is a good day for a celebration to conclude the season of Christmas in style. This is perhaps the best day for the wearing of paper crowns (either from Christmas crackers reserved for this party or home-made from heavy paper and brightly coloured stickers). Cakes decorated to look like crowns are another way of putting across the message that the Magi were recognizing Christ's kingship.

- *Blessing of the home*: There is a Roman Catholic tradition of blessing homes on Epiphany. This could be adapted for use in family celebrations at Epiphany. Why not process from room to room of your home, giving thanks for each room and the activities that go on there, and asking God to be present in those activities throughout the coming year. For further details on the blessing of homes, see Chapter 10. Why not combine this with the party? Or, if several members of a housegroup were to agree, you could all go from house to house, praying for each in turn, and finishing with a pot-luck supper.

- *Flowers for Epiphany*: Why not make a simple flower arrangement to reflect the theme of Epiphany? One way would be to pick flowers whose colours suggest the gifts of the wise men. Gold might be represented by chrysanthemums; frankincense by flowers or foliage in which blue, grey or silver predominate (e.g. eucalyptus leaves or the foliage of some conifers); myrrh by the colour traditionally associated with death, purple (e.g. by using an African violet in the foreground of your arrangement).

- *Family prayers for Epiphany*: Family worship on Epiphany might consist of a re-enactment of the journey of the Magi with everyone joining in to play different parts while one person narrates the story. With older children you might like to use T. S. Eliot's poem 'The Journey of the Magi'. Or you could, as we do, make the procession of the Magi figures to your nativity scene the focal point of family worship (perhaps accompanied by the singing of 'We Three Kings').

SPECIAL OCCASIONS BETWEEN EPIPHANY AND LENT

St Paul's Day (25th January)

This is the day on which Christians have traditionally celebrated the conversion of St Paul (he also shares a day with St Peter on 29th June).

Reading: Acts 9.1–22 (the story of Paul's conversion and call)
Song: 'Forth in thy name, O Lord, I go' (AMNS 239, MP 159)
            'God forgave my sin' (MP 181, SOF 129)
            'O Jesus, I have promised' (AMNS 235, MP 501, SOF 418)
Prayer: 'Almighty God, we thank you for enabling Paul to bring the light of the gospel into so many lives. As we celebrate his conversion, help us to follow him in bearing witness to the truth. Amen.'

Week of Prayer for Christian Unity

This is usually the week which includes St Paul's Day, although some churches celebrate it between Ascension and Pentecost. During the week, Christians of different denominations come together to hold joint meetings and acts of worship. Why not take this opportunity to worship with Christians from other traditions or invite someone from another church to a meal?

Why not explore a different tradition of Christian prayer in your family prayers? For example, if your tradition normally stresses spontaneous prayer, you might like to experiment with a prayer book from some other tradition (the Antiochian Orthodox Church, for instance, publishes an English language *Pocket Prayer Book for Orthodox Christians*).

Readings: At some point during the week, it would be a good idea to read through John 17. Jesus' high-priestly prayer is one of the key biblical texts underlying concern for Christian unity.
Songs: 'As we are gathered' (MP 38, SOF 28)
            'Bind us together' (JP 17, MP 54, SOF 43)
            'Brother, let me be your servant' (SOF 54)
            'Jesus put this song into our hearts' (MP 376, SOF 299)
            'Jesus stand among us' (SOF 303)
Prayers: Why not take time to pray for Christians who belong to different churches and traditions?

The Presentation of Christ in the Temple (2nd February)

Many people think that Christmas finishes with Epiphany. In fact, in the liturgical calendar, the end of the Christmas cycle is marked by Candlemas, which falls on the fortieth day after Christmas Day. Strictly speaking this is the festival of the Presentation of Christ in the Temple. It celebrates the day on which Joseph and Mary brought the infant Jesus to the Temple to be dedicated to God in accordance with Jewish custom (Lev. 12.1–8).

The name 'Candlemas' comes from the custom of blessing candles for use in church services on this day. Making candles a strong feature of this festival draws attention to the words of Simeon that here is 'a light for revelation to the Gentiles and for glory to your people Israel' (Luke 2.32).

Setting: We sometimes use Rembrandt's *Simeon and the Christ Child in the Temple* as a focal point for our prayers. It was the last of his paintings and was left unfinished when he died. It beautifully captures the relationship between the old man and the child, between death and life.

Reading: If you want to use this as your theme today, you might like to read the account in Luke 2.22–39.

Songs: 'Of the Father's love begotten' (AMNS 33)
             'Take my life, and let it be' (AMNS 249, MP 624, SOF 519)

Prayers: 'Lord, as you were presented in the Temple, help us to give ourselves wholly to you. Amen.
             Lord, let your light shine in our hearts today and every day. Amen.'

● *Making a Christingle*: As you may know, a Christingle (meaning 'Christ-light') is an orange with a red ribbon wrapped around its centre, a lighted candle in the top, and four cocktail sticks bearing nuts and dried fruit around the candle. Here is what the Children's Society says about the symbolism:

> The orange represents the world. Four sticks pressed into it represent the seasons, the fruits are the fruits of the earth, and the nuts on the sticks, the food we eat. The red ribbon represents our redemption through the blood of Christ and the lighted candle in the top of the orange symbolizes Jesus, the Light of the World.

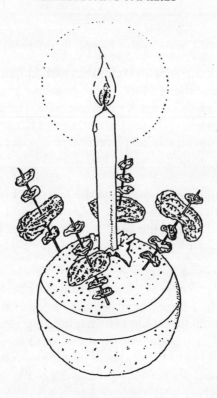

They play a central role in the increasingly popular Christingle service. This tradition originated in Moravia and was introduced to the Church of England as recently as 1968. If your local church does not yet hold a Christingle service or holds it early during the Advent-Christmas season, making Christingles and putting them in your windows is a good way of celebrating Candlemas as a family.

It is easy to make your own. For each Christingle, you will need

        1 orange
        1 candle
        a small piece of aluminium foil
        red ribbon (or sticky tape)
        a handful of raisins
        peanuts (in their shells)
        4 cocktail sticks

Wrap the ribbon (or tape) around the centre of the orange. Make a hole in the top of the orange. Wrap foil around the base of the candle and insert into hole. Thread the raisins and nuts on to the cocktail sticks. Push the sticks into the orange around the candle.

- *Candlemaking*: Candlemas seems an appropriate time for family activities like candlemaking (see 'Easter candles', p. 94). If your children are too young to handle molten wax safely, they can still make imitation candles from tightly rolled up lengths of wallpaper, topped with a cut out 'flame'. Alternatively, they can decorate ready-made candles with paints, ribbons, sticky-paper shapes, glitter, etc.

- *A Candlemas party*: Children love candles, so make sure there are plenty on the table. You could also decorate the room with snowdrops (they are sometimes called Candlemas Bells).

You can make a seasonal cake by turning a Swiss roll into a candle. Stand the cake on its end and cover it with marzipan, and then decorate it with fondant or butter icing. Reserve a small piece of marzipan for the flame and use food colouring to colour it red.

Since Simeon and Anna were both elderly, why not invite grandparents or elderly friends to this party? You might also like to use this occasion for a celebration of your baptisms or dedication to God.

St Valentine's Day (14th February)

Some readers may be surprised to find this day in a book on celebrating the Christian year. If anything, St Valentine's Day has been even more secularized than Christmas. For most people all vestiges of a Christian origin have been obscured by the sentimentalism of Valentine cards and silly messages in the personal columns of the newspapers. The Church seems to have abandoned the celebration of St Valentine and left it as an entirely secular festival.

Who was St Valentine? Apparently the early church used the day to celebrate two martyrs of this name. One was a Roman priest executed during the Claudian persecution of AD 269. The other was a bishop, also executed in Rome. As usual, legends abound about their deaths. It is said of the former Valentine (undoubtedly as a rationalization of his connection with lovers) that the crime for which he was executed was that of offering Christian marriage at a time when marriage had been banned by the emperor.

The most probable reason for fixing 14th February as St Valentine's Day was that it was the eve of the Lupercalia, a particularly wild Roman festival. It is often suggested that the early church hit on the festival of St Valentine as a way of redeeming a festival in honour of love. As we have said earlier, Christians have the choice of rejecting or redeeming the celebrations which are a part of their culture. Like the Christians of the early church we favour the latter strategy.

- *Valentine cards*: Sending Valentine cards is an important part of the tradition. But it is worth taking a critical look at the message: we can begin to do our bit in redeeming the day by rejecting any that are oversentimental or in bad taste. Alternatively you may prefer to make your own Valentine card.

  And why limit Valentine cards to our husbands or wives, or girl or boyfriends? Although it is primarily a celebration of romantic love we need not restrict ourselves to that. Why not send cards to others we love? For example, we could give cards to every member of our family (perhaps, including a sentence or verse celebrating something we like about that person). And on a day which can be particularly hard on those who are single, bereaved, or lonely perhaps we should make a special effort to remember such as are known to us.

- *Valentine tree*: This is an American idea inspired by the Advent custom of the Jesse tree. The day before St Valentine's Day every member of the family makes a paper heart. Then, in secret, they each think of some unselfish act of love which they can perform in the next twenty-four hours. The hearts are hung on a small branch in a weighted jam jar or flower pot. By the end of St Valentine's Day the branch will be decked with hearts representing some of the practical expressions of our love for each other.

- A *Valentine's Day walk*: St Valentine is also the patron saint of songbirds, making his festival an appropriate day to celebrate the first signs of new life in the new year. Why not go for a walk together? In medieval times it was thought that birds began mating on this day, so keep an eye open for any signs of birds beginning to build their nests. If it is too cold to go for a walk you could remember the birds and put out something for them to eat. Then they too will have something to enjoy and sing about!

- A *St Valentine's Day party*: It is a good day for a party; an excuse to dress up and enjoy some party food. Such a party is a way of saying 'I love you' to all the other members of your family.

    You could bake heart-shaped biscuits or make heart-shaped sandwiches. Some years ago we invested in a heart-shaped cake tin which comes into its own every 14th February. The children could be enlisted to make special decorations. Red and white are the traditional colours. Decorate the house with hearts, paper chains, balloons, flowers, etc. Get everyone involved in the preparations. Choose everyone's favourite food.

- *Valentine's Day charades*: Each person takes a turn to act out the identity of another family member. The actor begins by saying 'Who do I love?' and then has one minute to depict the chosen person. Everyone else tries to guess the identity. The one who guesses correctly takes the next turn and so on until everyone has had a turn. More difficult versions can be created by allowing players to choose a friend or relative who is not present, or by choosing Bible characters ('Who does God love?').

- *Family prayers on St Valentine's Day*: This seems a good day to focus on the love at the heart of the Christian gospel.

Readings: Suitable Bible readings include 1 Cor. 13; Luke 10.25–37 (the Good Samaritan); Luke 15.11–32 (the Prodigal Son); Ruth 1.6–18 (Ruth and Naomi); or 2 Sam. 4.4 and 9.1–13 (David and Jonathan). Alternatively, a modern story expressing Christian love might be used (e.g. Jennifer Gubb's *Wayne Hoskins and the Pram Lady* (Cambridge: Meridor Books, 1989)).

Songs: 'A new commandment' (MP 1, SOF 22)
'Come down, O love divine' (AMNS 156, MP 89)
'God is love: let heav'n adore him' (AMNS 365, MP 187)
'Love beyond measure' (SOF 375)

'Love divine' (AMNS 131, MP 449, SOF 377)

Prayer: 'Lord of love, forgive us when we fail to love. Give us your love that we may learn to love you in those around us and that you may love them through us. Amen.'

4
Lent

THE MEANING OF LENT

In terms of time, Lent is the single longest period within the Church's year. However, unlike most other seasons, it is not one we tend to look forward to. It conjures up images of fasting, of self-discipline, of mortification. We still talk of giving up something for Lent (even if it is only giving up 'giving up').

And yet it is of great symbolic importance. Coming as it does immediately before Easter, it gives expression to Jesus' fundamental manifesto of the Kingdom: 'Unless a grain of wheat falls into the ground and dies, it remains only a single seed' (John 12.24).

The forty days of the Lenten fast recall the forty years of wandering in the wilderness before the Israelites were able to take possession of the Promised Land. They recall the forty days spent by Jesus fasting and being tempted before the beginning of his earthly ministry. They also recall the period of Jesus' final journey to Jerusalem, his betrayal, crucifixion, and resurrection. Lent is not a time of asceticism for its own sake. It is not even a matter of giving up things *for* Jesus. On the contrary, during Lent we embark on a journey of preparation *with* Jesus.

It is a time when we can re-evaluate our Christian discipleship. It is the time when, traditionally, Christians have focused intensively on disciple-ship. Since the image of a journey is often associated with being a disciple (Jesus called us to take up our crosses and follow in his footsteps) that imagery is particularly appropriate at this time of year. In Lent we pay particular attention to our journey in the footsteps of Jesus. For adults this may have particular implications in the area of moral re-evaluation of our lifestyle. But the image of Lent as a time of mortification and penance is no more than a negative image created by mistaken views of discipleship.

We should not attempt to impose adult understandings of discipleship on young children. Rather we may stress the positive aspect of Lent by speaking of Jesus as our friend. Even this concept is beyond the understanding of a toddler (for whom another child is more likely to be a rival competing for a favourite toy). However, once they have reached playschool age children do have a basic idea of what friendship is. This is something to explore with them. Ask them how they feel about acting the same way or playing with their friends. Talk about helping each other.

The basic idea behind Lent can be conveyed to young children by telling them that, during Lent, we think especially about how God wants us to love each other. How do we know what we should do? Jesus came to show us. This can be illustrated by re-telling some of the incidents from the Gospels (such as when little children were brought to him; or the feeding of the five thousand). In what follows we shall build up a family Lent around the image of the Good Shepherd.

PREPARING FOR LENT: SHROVETIDE

Most people will probably be familiar with the tradition of making pancakes on Shrove Tuesday. In fact, many people think of it merely as Pancake Day. The origin of this traditional fare was the need to clear the larder of dairy products which might not be eaten during the Lenten fast.

Fewer people know that Shrove Tuesday was originally the climax of a three-day period of celebration known as Shrovetide. It began with the preceding Sunday (Quinquagesima Sunday). Shrove Monday (or Collop Monday) was the day on which all meat left in the larder would be used up. On Shrove Tuesday, as we have said, all fats and cream had to be used up (in France it is known as *Mardi Gras*: 'Fat Tuesday').

A simple pancake recipe

    4 oz (125 g) plain flour
    2 eggs
    ½ pint (300 ml) milk
    1 tbsp (15 ml) vegetable oil
Put all the ingredients into a bowl and whisk vigorously to make a smooth batter.

Heat a little oil in a frying pan, coat the base of the pan with about 30 ml batter, and cook until the top surface has just set. Toss (or flip the pancake with a fish-slice) and cook the other side until golden.

Work through all the batter in this way (adding a little more oil to the pan before each pancake). The pancakes can be kept warm in an oven until cooking is complete.

Pancakes may be served with a tremendous variety of savoury or sweet fillings (from tuna fish to ice cream). A favourite traditional way of serving is sprinkled with caster sugar and lemon juice.

Carnival

Since so much good food had to be consumed in a relatively short period it is hardly surprising that Shrovetide became a time of feasting and jollification. This is the period known in many parts of the world as 'Carnival' (*carni vale*: goodbye to meat).

Carnival is an opportunity to set aside our adult inhibitions. Masks, music and dancing enable us to get in touch with the child-like aspect of our personalities. It is a time when our usual responsibilities can be suspended. The Cadiz Carnival was banned for several years during the dictatorship of General Franco because of the tradition of singing satirical songs critical of the government.

During Carnival we celebrate the child-like in compensation for the seriousness of Lent. Some modern commentators see this in Jungian terms as an admission and expression of the dark, mysterious, unknown elements of the soul. In Christian terms it anticipates the child-likeness that Jesus said was characteristic of life in the Kingdom. It hints at the carefree playfulness and creativity which are to mark our relationship with the risen Lord.

It is an opportunity to let anarchy reign within the family: to permit a temporary relaxation of the usual order of the household. In our own family we restrict the anarchy to Tuesday itself. The Sunday is used to prepare for the celebrations of Monday and Tuesday. We choose a theme for our celebrations and organize whatever we may need. Do pictures need to be drawn or costumes contrived? On Collop Monday we have a feast of beefburgers to recall the way our ancestors cleared the larder of meat.

But Shrove Tuesday is the climax. In addition to pancakes, doughnuts will be on the menu at some point during the day. We all dress up and clown about (a dressing-up box is an asset in any household with children – our own includes several red noses, a couple of wigs, and a luminous green fur fabric coat). Face paints will be helpful in making the dressing up complete. Music is essential – Lawrence's personal favourite for this crazy celebration is part of Stravinsky's ballet *Pulcinella* (a hilarious tuba piece which sounds like a *pas de deux* for a pair of hippos) or we make our own music with the box of toy instruments at our disposal.

If you can face it, some degree of role reversal is appropriate. Hand over to the children some of the responsibility of running the household – let them choose the menus, etc. Conversely, give them something to think about by imitating some of their behaviour.

ASH WEDNESDAY

Ash Wednesday is the first day of Lent and, by tradition, a time of repentance.

In many churches ashes made by burning the previous year's palm crosses are distributed on this day. The priest makes the sign of the cross in ash on the forehead of each member of the congregation. One of the traditional formulae used at this signing sums up the significance of the day: 'Repent, and believe in the gospel.'

If it is impossible for the whole family to get to such a service, why not hold a simple service at home? In addition to (or instead of) last year's palm crosses, you can make ashes from pieces of paper on which you have written or drawn symbols of areas in your life where you want to exercise greater self-control. If you do decide to burn some old palm crosses you will find that they are extremely difficult to ignite – a little cooking oil, lighter fuel, or methylated spirits will help.

In our household we gather the family together before tea. After a reading of Joel 2.12–18 or Matt. 6.1–6, 16–18, those who are old enough take a few minutes to write or draw the areas they want to work on. This is done individually and the papers are folded so that other members of the family cannot see what each person has written. These are placed in an old tin along with any palm crosses we have found around the house and some cooking oil. Since it is probably dark by this time, we light the contents of the tin outside and retire indoors for tea. When the ashes are cool they may be mixed with a little water to make a suitable paste.

During evening prayers, we mark each others' foreheads saying 'Repent and receive the Good News.' This may be done by the leader, a parent, or by passing the tin round the circle and each marking the next person. At the end we say together 'God forgive us, and help us to do better in the future.'

Since Ash Wednesday marks the beginning of Lent, today is a good time to make a calendar together. With such a calendar we can chart our progress through Lent. Some suggestions for Lenten calendars are given in the section on Lenten activities.

LENTEN DISCIPLINE

Lent is a time of discipline. As we follow in Jesus' footsteps, we may choose to exercise Christian disciplines with particular intensity during this period. In particular, Christians have traditionally made it a time of prayer, fasting, and alms-giving.

The beginning of Lent may be an appropriate time to review our prayer life both in private and as a family. We may want to change our pattern of family prayers to reflect the season. For example, we may feel that it is appropriate to increase the time we devote to family prayers or to put more emphasis on self-examination and penitence.

Another area we might look at is the grace used at meals. Why not ask your children to compose a special Lenten grace? If they are older they could be encouraged to write down favourite verses from the Bible, put them all in a box, and read one at the beginning of each meal.

Lent may also be reflected in family reading. If you read together as a family why not select something appropriate to the season? For example, you might like to read part of *Pilgrim's Progress* every day.

Giving up something for Lent

A good deal could be said about fasting. Perhaps the most important point is that it is more than giving up some luxury for its own sake. Lenten fasting is better regarded as an intensification of ongoing efforts to live a simpler lifestyle.

The other side of fasting is alms-giving. Our giving up should not be entirely negative or self-centred. For example, giving up cigarettes simply for the attendant health benefits would be something. But if we pocketed the money saved we would have benefited only ourselves. What we save could be better used to help others. What we discover we can do without may be useful to someone else.

We usually think of money when we think of alms-giving. But again this is not all that this aspect of Lenten discipline need be about. We also give when we pay particular attention to the things we can do or the ways we can behave to enrich family life and the lives of our neighbours. Thus alms-giving can extend to patience, empathy, understanding, tolerance, creativity, humour, and joy. Lent is a particularly appropriate time for seeking God's grace that we may grow in the fruit of the Spirit.

Peace and quiet

Another aspect of Lenten discipline is the need for desert stillness. There should be space and silence. How about giving up some of those television programmes! Joan Halmo comments, 'the invitation is to travel light, leaving behind extra activities, some social engagements, some professional overtime – or, boldly now, all of them.'[1] A very encouraging example of that was the English diocese which gave up meetings for Lent one year!

Visual reminders of Lent

If you maintain a prayer corner in your living-room it may be set out as a visual reminder of the disciplines associated with Lent. An open Bible (perhaps open at the Gospel reading for the week) in a central position will serve as a reminder of the importance of prayer. If there are young children in the family a picture Bible would be most appropriate. A money box next to it could be used to collect our Lenten savings and thus serve as a reminder of the place of alms-giving. Children might be encouraged to decorate it with pictures relevant to our giving. For example, we often use photographs sent to us by missionary friends for this purpose. Similarly an empty wooden bowl may be used to recall that this a season of fasting and greater simplicity. Finally a cactus is a striking visual symbol of the desert, reminding us that during Lent we journey with Jesus in the wilderness.

If a prayer corner is not a normal part of your household, you might like to set one up specifically for Lent. Or you may prefer to use these symbols elsewhere in the house. Other possibilities for symbolizing Lent include replacing your usual table-cloth or place-mats with a piece of hessian.

Food for Lent

It is traditional to give up meat during Lent. Since in our family we have relatively little meat in our diet we opt for a simpler (but still wholesome) diet during Lent. However, we do make exceptions – if we are invited out, or when we find that we have guests.

Simple food should be the norm. Money saved can be put in the family money box and used for alms-giving. (By the way, it is a nice idea to pray for the people to whom our money will be going. Information and visual aids are easily obtainable from missionary societies, many of which now produce Lenten project packs.)

What about finding out what a typical meal would be in some part of the Third World? Christian Aid, Traidcraft, and Oxfam are all sources from which you may be able to obtain suitable recipes. Try some of them as family meals during Lent. This could be an interesting project for older children who could also be encouraged to find out how the food is produced.

Such Lenten simplicity can become the basis for a longer-term process of education in nutrition, stewardship, and responsible consumption (using your purchasing power to encourage socio-economic justice). Young children will simply absorb such concepts if they grow up in homes where they are consistently practised. There is no need to go into great detail or lecture them.

A simple diet during Lent also saves time since suitable meals will require less preparation (use slow-cooker meals, or one-dish dinners such as macaroni cheese). This time can be used for family projects, for reading, or for prayer.

Some Lenten recipes

- *Lentil stew*: In some countries it is the tradition to serve certain foods only in Lent. A modern variation on this might be to choose one particular dish as a reminder of Lent and serve it weekly, e.g. the following lentil stew (lentils were popular in Jesus' time and they recall the sound of the word 'Lent').

2 large onions	1 pint (570 ml) stock
1 clove garlic	1 14 oz (400 g) tin tomatoes
4 tbsp (60 ml) oil	2 carrots
8 oz (225 g) lentils	1 apple

Chop the onions and sauté in the oil with the crushed garlic clove until transparent. Wash and drain the lentils and add to the onions. Cook for 1 minute. Stir in the stock and tomatoes, bring to the boil, and boil the mixture for 5 minutes. Dice the carrots, chop the apple and stir into the lentils. Transfer to a slow cooker for 3 to 4 hours (on high).

- *Lenten pretzels*: Pretzels actually have a direct historical connection with Lent. It is thought they originated in the fifth century AD as a special Lenten bread. Since the Lenten fast ruled out dairy products, bread had to be made from flour, water and salt.

  The following is a very simple recipe; children are quite capable of assisting in its production.

6 oz (175 g) wholemeal flour	2 oz (50 g) butter
1 tsp (5 ml) salt	4 fl oz (125 ml) buttermilk
½ tsp (2 ml) baking soda	1 large egg

Mix together the flour, salt and baking soda. Add the butter and combine thoroughly. Add the buttermilk and egg, and mix well.

  Turn out on to a floured board, and knead until smooth and elastic. Roll out into 8″ long strands. Fold these into suitable shapes (such as crosses or other Christian symbols) and place on a greased tray. Sprinkle with sesame seeds. Bake at 200°C/Gas Mark 6 for 10 minutes.

- *Lenten kedgeree*: The following very simple fish dish omits the eggs which are usual in a kedgeree.

Boil up a pan of rice. Mix in a tin of tuna fish and some sweetcorn or peas.

LENT AND CHILDREN

Is it appropriate to keep Lent with young children? Many child develop-ment experts would question the wisdom of emphasizing the moral and dogmatic aspects of Lent. One Roman Catholic expert suggests that it may disrupt the foundations for later spiritual and moral development. This is because early childhood is seen as 'a time for growing in awareness of gifts given, a time of delight in the possession of love, a time of happiness in secure relationships. It is a time to know the Lord and rejoice in his presence.'[2]

Clearly this concern can be overdone. But it has had the good effect of encouraging people to look afresh at the positive aspects of Lent. It is not a matter of self-discipline for its own sake. Jesus' wilderness experience was not merely about resisting temptation. It was also a period in which he explored the possibilities for his ministry and opted for those which would deepen his pilgrimage with God the Father. Similarly we may see Lent as a time of exploration, with a view to deepening our own walk with God in a way that is appropriate to our state of life.

The Good Shepherd: a Lenten project

Halmo suggests that, for young children, Lent is a good time for coming to know Jesus as the Good Shepherd. This can be a helpful unifying theme for keeping Lent with young children. Rather than overloading children with many images, selecting just one allows them time and space to appreciate, pray, and contemplate a particular image.

The image of the Good Shepherd also forms a basis for understanding the significance of Easter: the three days of Easter being the time when the Good Shepherd gave his life for his sheep, and the subsequent period until Pentecost as a celebration of that gift to his flock.

- A prayer for Lent
  Thank you, Father, for your Son, Jesus the Good Shepherd. Thank you that he is our friend and shows us how to love others. Help us to be like him, kind to everyone we meet and good helpers, too.

Lent 1

During the first week of Lent the materials may be collected. These will include images or models of the Good Shepherd, sheep, and the sheepfold. Encourage your children to draw and cut out these images or use the small plastic models which are easily obtainable from toyshops. Another possibility would be to make the shepherd and his sheep in much the same way as was suggested for the Christmas crib. Remember that they are likely to see considerable use, so it is worthwhile taking time to make them really well.

Let the children use these images or models to re-enact the story of the Good Shepherd. As they play let them use their imagination to

work out how the shepherd would look after each of his sheep. Leave the models where the children can play with them whenever they want. In this way, their play helps to reinforce the story. Thus one child might have the shepherd kiss the sheep goodnight. Another might re-enact the daily activity of leading the sheep to water and pasture.

Lent 2
With the models made it is time to present the parable itself. The models should be ready to hand so that they can be used during the storytelling.

Introduce the parable by telling the children that Jesus called himself the Good Shepherd. Then tell the story. It is probably better to use one of the many children's Bible stories now available than the text of the Bible itself (at least with very young children). Ask them questions as you read – this will help them to get involved in the story. Perhaps you could conclude by lighting a candle and reading one of the Good Shepherd sayings from John's Gospel (John 10.3–5, 11, 14–16).

Afterwards, invite the children to retell the story in their own words. Ask them to think about who the sheep are.

One of the very helpful things about this parable for young children is the possibility of them discovering that there is a Good Shepherd who is stronger than the wolves and monsters which populate their imaginations and dreams. (This discovery helped our eldest daughter to stop having nightmares about General Wound-wort, the evil rabbit in *Watership Down*.)

Lent 3
Reinforce the parable and learn a song. Perhaps the first verse of Psalm 23 could be learned together.

Lent 4
Having established in their minds the image of the Good Shepherd, it is time to introduce the story of the lost sheep. Again, invite the children to retell the story and reflect on some aspects of it by asking simple questions. Our favourite version for children is the one in the Palm Tree Bible Story series.

Lent 5
Invite your children to make a picture of some aspect of the Good Shepherd parable. An older child might want to produce a picture-book about the parable.

Lent 6
Now is the time to link the idea of the Good Shepherd with the events of Easter. You can introduce the idea of the Good Shepherd being prepared to give his life for his sheep. It is time to reflect on the extent of the Shepherd's love and time for prayer.

OTHER LENTEN ACTIVITIES

A Lenten tree

This is a Lenten equivalent of the Advent Jesse tree. Each week during Lent, the children can be encouraged to draw pictures of the week's Gospel reading. Those pictures can be hung on a suitable branch.

One way of doing this would be to read the week's Gospel together. Spend some time thinking about the passage and praying. Then let the child get on with the picture. This reading/reflection/drawing may take place during the day or two after the Sunday.

Another possibility is to draw stained-glass pictures by using felt-tips on heavy plastic sheets. These may then be hung in a window.

Simplifying your life

With its emphasis on simplicity, Lent is a good time for attacking the clutter which threatens to swamp any household in which there are children. Give away unwanted toys or household goods. We keep our children's art-work on the kitchen walls. Lent is a good time for replacing that which has been there for a while.

Pare down; eliminate things that are now superfluous. Take a critical look at your bookshelves or your wardrobes. Is there anything that you really do not need? In addition, it may be helpful to put away some of the more decorative items in your home (these may be brought out again when Easter arrives).

A Lenten calendar

Lent is a journey, so why not draw a calendar which reflects that? A sheet of A3 cartridge paper would be suitable (or a length of old wallpaper). Draw paving stones for each day of Lent. Remember that the Sundays during Lent are not counted towards the forty days; they could be made larger and outlined in a different colour. Cut out a figure for each child and mount it on card. These can be attached to the first paving stone with blue tack. Each day the children can move their own figure along one space. When you reach a Sunday fill it in with a picture related to the Gospel reading that day. You can do the same for any other important days during Lent and Holy Week.

Alternatively the children can be encouraged to make a Lenten paper-chain. One link is added each day. After they have gone to bed on Easter Eve, attach cardboard butterflies to the ends of their chains (symbolizing new life) and put them up as decorations for Easter Day.

Sharing and giving

This need not be money. Time, attention, care, forgiveness, love: all these are for giving.

Why not adopt a grandparent? This might involve encouraging members of the family to visit an older person regularly during Lent. They could take some home-made Lenten food with them. They could also be encouraged to pray regularly for the people they visit.

Or try sharing more within the family. Ideas for family sharing projects include planting seeds together, or making Easter cards. Another possibility is a remembering time: everyone brings along a photograph, scrapbook or some object which can be used as the inspiration for talking about 'I remember when . . .'

Banner making

Another form of visual display for Lent would be a home-made banner or poster. Create something which reflects the three-fold theme of prayer, fasting, and giving. Alternatively, a mask with half the face gloomy and the other half cheerful can be used as a reminder that Lent is not a dismal affair. Remember Jesus' advice, 'When you fast do not look like the hypocrites . . .'

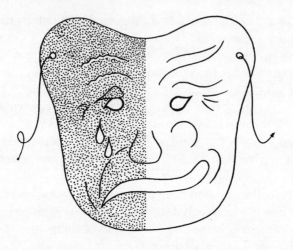

~~~~~~~~~~~~~~~~~~~~~~~~~~

SPECIAL OCCASIONS DURING LENT

Mothering Sunday

This is the fourth Sunday in Lent. The traditional theme for this Sunday originally developed from the Roman custom of honouring the goddess of motherhood at about this time. Instead of motherhood, medieval Christians celebrated Mother Church. It was a natural enough step to extend this celebration to include our natural mothers as well as our spiritual mother. By the eighteenth century it was customary for girls 'in service' to be allowed to go home for the day.

The custom was reinforced by the creation of Mothers' Day earlier this century in the USA. This originally had nothing to do with Mothering Sunday. However, many American servicemen stationed in Britain during the Second World War adopted their hostesses as foster mothers and gave them presents and flowers in appreciation of their hospitality. Soon the two days merged in most people's minds.

Many churches celebrate by distributing flowers to children in the congregation so that they may give them to their mothers. Daffodils are probably the most popular. Often real flowers are used but in some parishes artificial flowers have gradually been adopted. In our own parish, cloth flowers made by disabled people are used.

- *Celebrating Mothering Sunday in the home*: Father and children could take responsibility for the Sunday meals and prepare a special celebration for mum. Since Sundays are not counted in the forty days of Lent you will not be breaking any Lenten disciplines if you indulge yourselves today.

  Get the children to decorate a special place-setting for their mother. Put spring flowers on the dining table. Why not make her a posy with seasonal flowers (forsythia, daffodils, jonquils, polyanthus or jasmine) surrounded by a little greenery (box or ferns)?

- *Simnel cake*: This was the traditional gift for a daughter to give her mother on Mothering Sunday. The name is thought to come from *simila* – the Latin name for the very fine flour used in these cakes. It is still an appropriate culinary symbol for this day. Its distinguishing feature is a layer of marzipan baked inside it, and eleven marzipan eggs on top (to represent the apostles minus Judas).

6 oz (175 g) butter	1 lb (450 g) mixed dried fruit
6 oz (175 g) sugar	1 tsp (5 ml) cinnamon
2 or 3 eggs	1 tsp (5 ml) mixed spice
8 oz (225 g) self-raising flour	the juice, flesh and rind of 1 lemon

  Cream together the butter and sugar until soft and fluffy. Add the egg, and then the remaining ingredients and mix thoroughly.

  Line the bottom and sides of a large cake-tin with tin foil and grease it thoroughly. Put half the mixture in it.

  Roll out a packet of marzipan and cut out a circle to fit the cake-tin. Place this in the tin and add the remaining cake mix.

  Bake in a moderate oven (150°C/Gas Mark 2) for 3 hours, and then cover with grease-proof paper and bake for a further 30 minutes (or until a knife inserted into the cake comes out clean).

  Decorate with another circle of marzipan on the top and wide strips for the sides. Stick the marzipan to the cake with a generous layer of jam. Make up 11 marzipan eggs and put them round the top.

St David's Day (1st March)

There is little reliable information
about the patron saint of Wales.
David (or Dewi) was probably a
younger son of an aristocratic
British family and, hence, destined
from childhood for the Church. In
sixth-century Wales Christianity
was in conflict with the old religion
of the Britons. David is renowned
as a preacher of the gospel and
founder of monasteries. He finally
settled at Mynyw (now St David's).
According to legend the area
around St David's was terrorized by
a brigand named Boca. David
befriended him and he eventually
became a Christian. (If you or your
family enjoy fantasy novels,

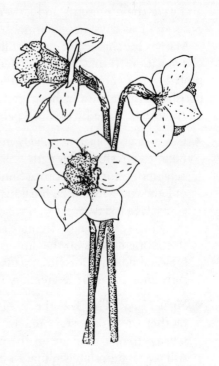

David appears as a character in *Taliesin* (Lion, 1988) and *Merlin* (Lion,
1988), the first two books of Stephen Lawhead's powerful Christian
synthesis of the legends of Atlantis and King Arthur.)

- *Bara brith*: Why not make this traditional Welsh bread to celebrate the
  patron of Wales?

1 lb (450 g) mixed dried fruit	1 tsp (5 ml) mixed spice
3 oz (75 g) sugar	2 tbsp (30 ml) marmalade
8 fl oz (225 ml) cold tea	1 egg
1 lb (450 g) self-raising flour	

  Mix the fruit, sugar and tea and leave to soak overnight. The next day,
  add the flour, mixed spice and marmalade. Stir the mixture, and then
  add the egg. Pour into a lined and greased 3 lb loaf tin and bake in a
  moderate oven (180°C/Gas Mark 4) for an hour and a quarter.

A couple of Welsh national symbols, the leek and the daffodil, are
often associated with St David's Day. The leek was worn as a battle
emblem by the Welsh. The daffodil, which is in flower at this time of year,
is sometimes known as David's flower. Why not work one or other into
your St David's Day celebrations?

Reading: 1 Thess. 2.2b–12 (the sentiments of Paul, Silas and
            Timothy but we may well imagine David making similar
            comments to the pagan Britons among whom he minis-
            tered).

Songs: 'Guide me, O thou great Jehovah' (AMNS 214, MP 201,
            SOF 148)

Prayer: 'Almighty God, we thank you for the example of David.
            Help us to be more like him in purity of life and enthusiasm
            for the gospel of Christ. Amen.'

St Patrick's Day (17th March)

Patrick, the patron saint of Ireland, lived before David (fifth century) but
we know a good deal more about him since some of his writings have
survived.

He was brought up as a Christian somewhere in Britain (towns as far
apart as Banwen in Wales and Old Kilpatrick in Scotland claim him as
their own). However, he did not take his faith seriously until he was
captured by Irish pirates at the age of sixteen. After six years in captivity
he escaped and made his way back to Britain where he trained for the
priesthood. Subsequently he returned to Ireland to bring the gospel to
those who had enslaved him. He spent the rest of his life in Ireland,
becoming the founder and first bishop of the Irish Church.

Why not find out more about the real Patrick by reading his *Confession?*
It is a short work and can be found in *Aristocracy of Soul: Patrick of Ireland*
(London, DLT, 1987) by Noel O'Donoghue. In it Patrick describes his
conversion and later return to Ireland as a missionary.

- *The shamrock:* The shamrock is recognized the world over as an emblem
  of Ireland. According to tradition, it is also closely associated with St
  Patrick. Apparently he was fond of using its three leaves springing from
  one stem as a visual image for the Trinity: three persons in one God.

  Why not decorate your home today with shamrocks cut from green
  paper (either individually or as paper-chains)? If you make a big
  enough shamrock, you could write in the persons of the Trinity on the
  three lobes.

Reading: Rom. 8.1–17, 28–30. (Judging by the frequency with
            which he quotes it, this was St Patrick's favourite book and
            these verses summarize the good news which he brought to
            the Irish people.)

Song: 'Be thou my vision' (AMNS 343, MP 51)

Prayer: 'Christ be with me, Christ within me,
               Christ behind me, Christ before me,
               Christ beside me, Christ to win me,
               Christ to comfort and restore me,
               Christ beneath me, Christ above me,
               Christ in quiet, Christ in danger,
               Christ in mouth of friend or stranger.'

                                    (*from* St Patrick's Breastplate)

Feast of the Annunciation (25th March)

This is exactly nine months before Christmas Day. At one time it was
known as Lady Day but its modern title is more descriptive. It is the day
when we remember how the Angel Gabriel came to Mary to announce
that she had been chosen to be the mother of Jesus.

Since angels are essentially messengers, members of the family might
celebrate this day by writing a letter or making a phone call to cheer
someone up.

Setting: Why not look in your box of Christmas decorations for a
               Christmas angel and a figure of Mary to act as the
               centrepiece for your prayers? Alternatively, you might use a
               reproduction of one of the many paintings of this event.
Prayer: 'Father, help us to follow Mary's example and respond
               obediently to your word that we might become messengers
               of good news like Gabriel. Amen.'
Reading: Luke 1.26–38.
Songs: 'How lovely on the mountains' (JP 84, MP 249, SOF 192)
               'Love divine, all loves excelling' (AMNS 131, MP 449,
               SOF 377)
               'Tell out my soul' (AMNS 422, JP 229, MP 631, SOF 520)

5
Holy Week

PRACTICAL PREPARATIONS

Holy Week is the heart of the Christian year. During this week Christians everywhere focus on the central events of the Gospels from Jesus' triumphal entry into Jerusalem to his arrest, crucifixion and resurrection. Thus it is appropriate to make it a central feature of our life together as a family. In our hyper-active culture this may mean preparing for it in advance.

Schedules

We may want to arrange for time off work during Holy Week to celebrate with our family and local church (particularly if Good Friday to Easter Day are normally working days for us). Within the home, we may want to reschedule housework so that what would normally be done between Thursday and Sunday is moved into the first half of the week.

Meals

As the greatest celebration of the Christian year, Easter Day surely deserves to be marked by a party comparable with those we traditionally hold at Christmas. As with Christmas this will require some planning and advance preparation. Some Christians also like to have a special meal on Maundy Thursday to recall the Last Supper. Ideas for recipes can be found later in the chapter.

By contrast, simple meals are more appropriate for Good Friday and Holy Saturday (and, since they are technically part of Lent, for the Monday to Wednesday of Holy Week).

Something new for Easter?

The tradition of buying new clothes for Easter is a visible reminder of the new life which Jesus brought by dying and rising for us and which we have put on in baptism. It need not be anything as extravagant as a new suit of clothes. Some token (e.g. a new necklace, hairband, or tie) is enough.

A calendar for Holy Week

Sunday	Jesus enters Jerusalem	
Monday	Jesus ejects the money changers and traders from the Temple; the religious leaders plot against him	
Tuesday	Jesus is anointed at Bethany	
Wednesday	Jesus continues to teach in Temple in spite of growing opposition from the authorities	
Thursday	*(late afternoon)*	The Last Supper
	(evening)	Jesus is arrested
	(night)	The trial
Friday	*(early morning)*	Jesus before Pilate
	(late morning)	Jesus is taken to be executed
	(noon)	The crucifixion
	(3.00 p.m.)	Jesus dies
	(late afternoon)	Jesus is buried
Saturday	The disciples mourn	
Sunday	*(dawn)*	The tomb is empty; Jesus is risen!

This could be the basis for a wall calendar on which family members might be encouraged to put thoughts, prayers, or pictures for Holy Week.

Family reading for Holy Week

If you regularly read to your family, why not pick something appropriate to the season? For example,

> Sylvia Engdahl, *Heritage of the Star* (Puffin, 1976)
> Madeleine L'Engle, *A Wrinkle in Time* (Puffin, 1967)
> C. S. Lewis, *The Lion, the Witch and the Wardrobe* (Puffin, 1959)

> *Patricia St John, Jesus the King* (Scripture Union, 1991)
> E. B. White, *Charlotte's Web* (Puffin, 1963)
> Oscar Wilde, *The Selfish Giant* (Walker Books, 1986)

Or, for younger children:

> Eric Carle, *The Very Hungry Caterpillar* (Puffin, 1974)
> Caryll Houselander, *Petook: An Easter Story* (Burns & Oates, 1990)
> Margery Williams, *The Velveteen Rabbit* (Heinemann, 1970)

Music and pictures for Holy Week

Many artists and composers have been inspired by the events which we remember this week. Thanks to modern technology we can enjoy their work in our own homes. Why not display a print of an appropriate painting (or sculpture) in a prominent place this week? Why not choose a relevant piece of music and take time to become familiar with it?

- *Music for Holy Week and Easter*

J. S. Bach	*Easter Oratorio*
	St John Passion
	St Matthew Passion
Barber	*Agnus Dei*
Handel	*Messiah*
Poulenc	*Stabat Mater*
Rossini	*Stabat Mater*
Schütz	*Easter Oratorio*
Stainer	*Crucifixion*
Tavener	*The Ikon of the Crucifixion*
	The Repentant Thief

Johnny Cash	'Redemption' from *American Recordings*
Graham Kendrick	*Make Way for the Cross*
Stephen Schwartz	*Godspell*
Adrian Snell	*The Passion*
Andrew Lloyd Webber	*Jesus Christ Superstar*

- *Visual art*: The events of Holy Week have been a rich source of inspiration for many artists. A good collection of art and meditation relating to Good Friday is to be found in Hans-Ruedi Weber's *On a Friday Noon* (SPCK, 1979). Why not build up your own collection of prints and postcards relating to Holy Week? For example, the following are all to be found in British galleries:[1]

El Greco, *Christ Driving the Traders from the Temple*
Ford Madox Brown, *Christ Washing St Peter's Feet* (Tate)
Giovanni Bellini, *Agony in the Garden*
Gerrit van Honthorst, *Christ before the High Priest*
Diego Velasquez, *Christ after the Flagellation*
Hieronymus Bosch, *The Crowning with Thorns*
Austrian School, *The Trinity with Christ Crucified*
Salvador Dali, *Christ of St John of the Cross* (Kelvin, Glasgow)
Master of Liesborn, *Head of Christ Crucified*
Michelangelo, *The Entombment*
Rembrandt, *The Entombment of Christ* (Hunterian, Glasgow)

PALM SUNDAY

Many churches celebrate Jesus' entry into Jerusalem with processions and/
or by distributing palm crosses today. If you cannot share in such an event
why not have your own family procession?

Instead of palms you might cut branches from your garden or, if you can
get permission to cut them, twigs of willow catkin.[2] Alternatively, you
could get the children to make palm fronds from sheets of paper. Simply
roll up a large sheet of paper to form a tube and create the fronds by
making a series of cuts down the length of the tube.

Songs: 'All glory, laud and honour' (AMNS 60)
'Majesty, worship his majesty' (JP 160)
'Ride on, ride on in majesty!' (AMNS 61)
'The king of glory comes' (SOLW 124)
'We cry "Hosanna, Lord!"' (CH 132)
'We have a king who rides a donkey' (JP 264)
'You are the king of glory' (JP 296)

Reading: Matt. 21.1–11; Mark 11.1–10; or Luke 19.29–40
Alternatively you might prefer to read a modern re-telling
of the story, such as Margaret Gray's *The Donkey's Tale*
(Scripture Union, 1984) or Susan Sayers' *Jesus on a Donkey*
(Palm Tree Press, 1985).

Prayer: 'Lord Jesus, as you entered Jerusalem so enter our hearts and
home today. Help us to welcome you with truth and
sincerity, and teach us to walk in your way all the days of
our life. Amen.'

Holy Week frieze

On a large sheet of paper make a line drawing to represent Jerusalem with the Mount of Olives on one side and Golgotha and the Tomb on the other. Get the children to colour it in.

This can be used throughout Holy Week as a background on which to stick paper figures to represent the various events of the week. Today get the children to draw a picture of Jesus riding on a donkey and people waving palm branches.

MONDAY TO WEDNESDAY

A time of preparation

These last three days of Lent are a traditional time for spring cleaning. Perhaps we could revive this custom, taking time to go round the house, room by room, tidying and doing all those little (or big) cleaning jobs which tend to be overlooked in the regular pattern of housework. It is also a good time to prepare for the Easter celebrations, by doing some of the cooking for Easter Day.

Paradise torte

This is a rich cake of Eastern European origin which has to be made early in Holy Week in order to 'ripen' for Easter Day.

10 oz (275 g) butter	the grated rind of 1 lemon
1 lb 8 oz (675 g) sugar	1 lb (450 g) flour
1 whole egg	8 oz (250 g) marzipan (grated)
4 eggs (separated)	1 tsp (5 ml) cinnamon
½ tsp (2.5 ml) salt	1 pint (570 ml) whipping cream
flaked almonds to decorate	

Cream together butter and 1 lb of the sugar. Add the whole egg, 4 egg yolks, salt and lemon rind. Work in the flour to make a stiff dough. Divide into four 9-inch cake tins, completely covering the base of each.

Beat the egg whites until peaks form. Fold in the marzipan, remaining sugar and cinnamon. Divide into four and spread on top of each layer of dough. Bake at 180°C/Gas Mark 4 for 25–35 minutes or until cakes are golden brown.

Cool slightly but remove from tins while still warm.

Choose the layer with the best base and invert it to form the top.

Whip the cream, divide it into 3 and spread on each of the remaining layers. Put the inverted layer on top and press lightly to let the cream ooze out between the layers. Spread excess cream around sides and sprinkle with flaked almonds. Arrange it so that the meringue side is on the top, to retain meringue texture.

Keep in a cool place to ripen, checking daily. When it is soft and settled, put it in the refrigerator. Sprinkle with icing sugar before serving. Alternatively, you could reduce the quantities to two-thirds and the cream by half to make two smaller double-decker tortes.

Readings: Most lectionaries concentrate on the Passion narratives during Holy Week. For example, Monday: Matt. 26.1–30; Tuesday: Matt. 26.31–75; Wednesday: Matt. 27.1–54.

Alternatively, you may prefer to look at other aspects of Jesus' last week in Jerusalem during these three days. For example, Monday: Mark 11.12–19 (The cleansing of the Temple); Tuesday: Mark 12.28–34 (The great commandment); Wednesday: Mark 14.1–11 (The anointing at Bethany).

~~~~~~

MAUNDY THURSDAY

A simple footwashing ceremony

Before you sit down to dinner, mother or father could take a basin and wash everyone's feet. Another member of the family could read the relevant passage (John 13.3–17). Alternatively, several people could read, with one person taking the part of Jesus, another Simon Peter and a third narrating.

Prayer: 'Lord Jesus, enable us to be the servant of others as You were the servant of all. Amen.'

Song: 'A new commandment' (SOF 22, SOLW 66)[3]
'Broken for me, broken for you' (CH 68, SF 53)
'Brother, let me be your servant' (CH 70, SF 54)
'Make me a channel of your peace' (JP 161)
'The Song of the Supper'[4]

Re-enacting the Last Supper

Some Christians go to great lengths to reproduce a Jewish Passover meal.[5]
For others this is theologically dubious, or insensitive towards Jewish
friends, or simply too time-consuming. What follows is a much-simplified
version which stresses the innovation made by Jesus.

Lighting of candle(s) by mother:
> Blessed are you, Lord God, King of the universe, who
> has kept us alive and sustained us and brought us to this
> season. May our home be consecrated by the light of
> your countenance, shining upon us in blessing and
> bringing us peace.

Reading: Pss. 113, 114.

Blessing:
> Blessed are you, Lord God, King of the universe
> you bring forth bread from the earth.
>
> *All*: **Blessed be God for ever.**
>
> Blessed are you, Lord God, King of the universe
> you create the fruit of the vine.
>
> *All*: **Blessed be God for ever.**

The meaning of the bread and wine:
> *Child*: Why do we eat bread and drink wine tonight at
> this special meal?
>
> *Parent*: We do so because at the Last Supper our Lord
> took bread and wine and blessed them. As it is written
> . . . [the parent reads Luke 22.14–20 or Matt. 26.26–
> 29].

> *The meal*
> *Concluding Psalm*: Ps. 118
> *Dismissal*:   'When they had sung a hymn, they went out to the
>   Mount of Olives' (Matt. 26.30).

Traditional Passover food

You might like to introduce some of these into your Maundy Thursday
dinner. If you do so, it is a good idea to include an explanation of their
significance within the Passover meal.

Hard-boiled egg	the hardness of Pharaoh's heart; symbol of new life after deliverance
Roast lamb	the Passover meal (Ex. 12.8); Jesus, the Lamb of God
Matzoh	unleavened bread eaten in haste by the Israelites escaping from Egypt; the body of Christ
Maror	bitter herbs (e.g. horseradish); the bitter experience of slavery
Karpas	greens (e.g. parsley, watercress); new life
Salt water	a dip for the greens; the tears of the Israelites; the Red Sea (passage to freedom)
Charoseth	the clay of the bricks made by the Israelites in slavery; the sweetness and joy of deliverance
Red wine	the blood marking out the Israelite doorposts; the blood of Christ

- *Charoseth*:   1 apple, peeled, cored and finely chopped
  2 oz (50 g) finely chopped walnuts or almonds
  ½ tsp (2.5 ml) sugar
  ½ tsp (2.5 ml) cinnamon
  1 tbsp (15 ml) red wine

Mix together the apples, nuts, sugar and cinnamon. Add the liquid and
mix thoroughly.

Gethsemane

After the dismissal from the meal, why not re-enact the walk to
Gethsemane?

All: File out into the garden, perhaps singing a simple song, such as 'Kum-ba-yah' or 'We are marching in the light of God'.

Reading: Matt. 26.36–56; Mark 14.32–50; or Luke 22.39–53

Prayers: If you or your children feel self-conscious about praying aloud in the garden, you could ask them to write a simple prayer on a piece of card cut to look like a seed. That seed may be passed around and read in silence before being 'planted' by the child who wrote it.

Song: 'Stay here' (Taizé)[6]

If you do not have a garden or it is too wet or cold to venture outside, simply designate one of the rooms in your house or flat Gethsemane for this occasion.

GOOD FRIDAY

Today we remember Jesus' arrest, trial and crucifixion. Many churches hold acts of worship on Good Friday and it is more appropriate to meet together as the whole family of God than to have a privatized family act of worship. Nevertheless there are various things we can do at home to bring the significance of Good Friday to mind.

Hot cross buns

Traditionally these were eaten at breakfast on Good Friday. But they could be a part of any meal today. Here is a simple recipe.

8 oz (225 g) plain flour	1 egg
¼ tsp (1 ml) mixed spice	3 oz (75 g) currants
¼ pint (140 ml) milk	½ oz (15 g) mixed peel
½ oz (15 g) yeast	1 tbsp (15 ml) sugar boiled with milk
1½ oz (40 g) caster sugar	to glaze
2 oz (50 g) butter	

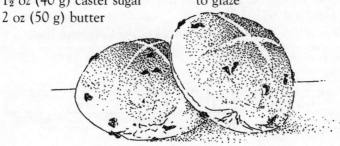

Warm the milk and the yeast gently until dissolved. Let it cool slightly and mix with rest of ingredients. Leave the dough to rise for an hour and a half in a warm place. Knock back and let rise for another 30 minutes. Form into 8 balls and let rise for another 15 minutes. Run a sharp knife across each bun to form the cross. Bake for 15 minutes in a pre-heated oven (220°C/Gas Mark 7). Cool and glaze.

As you eat the buns together it is worth thinking about their symbolism: the cross is a reminder of Jesus' death for us while the spices remind us of the spices used to prepare his body for burial.

Plant some seeds

This can be either an outdoor or an indoor activity. You should choose easy-to-grow varieties which will be reasonably tolerant of mistreatment, and let the children themselves have the fun of planting the seeds. For outdoor planting these might be candytuft, cornflower, godetia, nasturtiums, marigolds, or scabious. Relate the planting of the seeds to Jesus' saying about the grain of wheat (John 12.24).

Re-tell the story of the good shepherd

You may feel that it is not appropriate to describe the events of Good Friday to very young children. In this case, why not re-tell the story of the good shepherd who loves his sheep so much that he is prepared to die for them. If you used this theme during Lent you could dramatize the re-telling with the models your children made.

Make a cross

The above words of caution will not apply to older children. On the contrary, you should not try to play down the reality to which our Good Friday practices point. The horror of crucifixion lies at the heart of the Christian faith, though it has been transformed by its indissoluble connection with the miracle of resurrection. Thus an instrument of torture and execution has become a symbol of the Christian hope.

Making a cross from pieces of wood and nails is a graphic way of focusing upon this truth. Our making of the cross reminds us that, in a very real sense, our sins have helped to make the cross on which our Lord died. But at the same time it reminds us that, in accepting that fate, he turned things upon their head, wiping away our sins and holding out the sure promise of eternal life.

You could take this meditation a step further by actually hammering nails into the cross you have constructed. Alternatively, place the cross in a prominent position with several large nails next to it.

Easter garden

Children can be enlisted to construct a model garden in an old basin. All that is needed is some earth, a few rocks (to construct the tomb) and some moss and flowers or twigs from a bush. It will probably be necessary to supervise the collection of the raw materials (in order to prevent the possible destruction of a prize bush or the digging up of a square foot of lawn!). But once they have the raw materials, leave them to use their own imagination. If Good Friday is beginning to look rather busy, you might prefer to leave this activity for Saturday.

Reading: Matt. 27.33–56
Prayer: 'Jesus who died for me
            Help me to live for thee. Amen.'

Song: 'I danced in the morning' (JP 91)
'O sacred head, sore wounded' (AMNS 68)
'There is a green hill far away' (AMNS 137, JP 245)
'Were you there' (AMNS 523, JP 269)
'When I survey the wondrous cross' (AMNS 67, JP 277)

Prayer: 'Thanks be to thee,
Lord Jesus Christ,
for all the benefits
which thou hast won for us,
for all the pains and insults
which thou hast borne for us.
O most merciful Redeemer,
Friend and Brother,
may we know thee more clearly,
love thee more dearly,
and follow thee more nearly,
day by day.'
(Richard of Chichester)

SATURDAY/EASTER EVE

Today is a day of waiting and preparation for the feast of Easter. In many churches people will be busy decorating with flowers and making sure that everything is ready for the great celebration. At home, too, we may use the time for quiet preparation.

Decorating the house

You might like to prepare the house for tomorrow's party. Fresh flowers are the traditional form of decoration. These may be arranged on Saturday and left overnight in a cool place ready to be put in their proper positions early on Easter Sunday morning.

Decorating eggs

1. Simply hard boil a few eggs. Once they are cool they may be decorated using felt-tipped pens. Try to think of symbols associated with the Easter story (e.g. the cross; the rising sun; a butterfly). They can be placed in a bowl on your dining table until you are ready to eat them. (Why not make the eating of these special eggs a family tradition? For example, they could become the main course for breakfast on Easter Sunday.)

 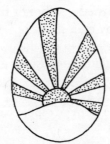 

2. A more elaborate procedure suitable for older children is to dye the eggs. Soak them in vinegar beforehand. This helps the shells to absorb the colours of the dyes. Boiling them with beetroot juice results in a pink stain while onion skins will give a yellow colouration. Quite elaborate patterns may be built up by waxing over the areas which you do not want to dye that particular colour.

3. Yet another option is to blow the eggs (puncturing the shell at top and bottom and removing the uncooked contents). The shell can then be given a coat of clear varnish and painted. This procedure has the advantage that the result is permanent. You can hang blown eggs by tying a length of cotton to a small piece of match stick and inserting the match stick into the egg.

4. You may like the idea of decorated eggs but shy away from the mess involved in decorating them yourself. If so, you might like to look out for special Easter egg wraps. These are decorated plastic sleeves which slip over and shrink to fit hot eggs. We first encountered them in North America but have subsequently found them in art shops in England.

Easter egg tree

Two or three hawthorn branches in a pot surrounded by spring flowers make a very effective table decoration from which to hang decorated eggs. Some families save the eggs they blow from year to year and so gradually build up large collections of eggs which can be hung in this way. A simpler alternative would be to hang small chocolate Easter eggs instead.

Easter candles

If you and your children enjoy candlemaking this is an obvious Easter Eve activity. If you have never tried it why not have a go? It is much easier than you might think. Many craft shops sell wax, wicks and moulds. Or you can re-use old candle ends, use heavy string for the wick and improvise a cylindrical mould from a washing-up liquid bottle.

---

1. Melt the old candle ends in an old saucepan or double-boiler and remove leftover wicks.
2. Dip the string or wick in the molten wax and lay aside on a sheet of newspaper.
3. Attach the wick through a hole in the bottom of the container and seal with plasticine. Tie the other end around a pencil and balance it across the top of the container to keep it centred. Place the container on newspapers (in case of spills).
4. Pour molten wax carefully into one container, taking care that the wick remains in the centre.
5. Leave the candle to cool for about 15 minutes and top up any hollow created by shrinkage.
6. Carefully remove the candle from mould.
7. Like Easter eggs you can decorate your candle with symbols relating to Easter. These might be transfers purchased from a candlemaking specialist or you could paint them on using poster paints.

The candle can become a centrepiece for your dinner table on Easter Sunday. If it is large enough you can light it every Sunday for many weeks. It is a reminder that Christ is the Light who has overcome the darkness in the world.

Easter biscuits

One old Easter tradition is to make biscuits and then give them away in bundles of three as a reminder of God the Father, Son, and Holy Spirit. Any recipe which contains spices will do. As with hot cross buns, the spices serve as a reminder of the spice which the women took to the tomb on the first Easter Sunday. Here is a traditional recipe from the West Country.

> 4 oz (115 g) butter
> 3 oz (85 g) caster sugar
> 1 egg (separated)
> 7 oz (200 g) plain flour
> pinch of salt
> ½ tsp (2.5 ml) mixed spice
> ½ tsp (2.5 ml) cinnamon
> 2 oz (50 g) currants
> 1 tbsp (15 ml) mixed peel
> 1–2 tbsp (15–30 ml) brandy or milk
> caster sugar for sprinkling

Cream the butter and sugar until pale and fluffy, and then beat in the egg yolk. Sift in the flour, salt and spices and mix well. Add the fruit and peel and enough brandy or milk to make a fairly soft dough.

Knead lightly and roll out until about a quarter of an inch thick. Cut into 2-inch rounds using a fluted cutter. Place on greased baking trays and bake at 200°C/Gas Mark 6 for 10 minutes.

Remove from the oven, brush with egg white, sprinkle with a little caster sugar and return to the oven for about 5 minutes (until the tops are golden brown). Cool on a wire rack.

Reading: Hosea 6.1–3
Prayer: 'Lord, we thank you that, through you, our times of waiting
                are filled with hope not despair. Help us to wait patiently
                for all the good things you have promised to your followers.
                Amen.'
Song: 'Watch and pray' (a simple chant of the Iona Community)

If your local church holds an Easter Vigil (and your children are old
enough to appreciate it) you might prefer to worship with your wider
Christian family this evening.

6
Easter

And so we come to the climax of the Christian year. Today we celebrate the heart of our faith; that which makes Christianity good news.

As with Christmas we will probably want to gather together with other members of the Christian family to celebrate Jesus' resurrection from the dead. However, it seems appropriate that the joy of Easter should spill over into all we do today.

In our family, one of the things we do to mark the newness of Easter is to provide everyone with something new to wear to church. Even a small item of clothing is enough to symbolize the newness of life after Easter. For example, our children are crazy about hats: last year, their Easter present was a new hat each which they wore proudly to church.

Sunday lunch on Easter Day is an ideal opportunity for a full-scale party. Party hats (or rather, Easter crowns) could be made for everyone to wear. As at Christmas, the children could be drafted in to make placemats (this time with Easter themes). Roast lamb is a good choice for the main course: it was an important part of the Jewish Passover meal but, more importantly, reminds us of Jesus, *our* Passover lamb. Be extravagant! This is the most important feast day in the Christian calendar! Make sure

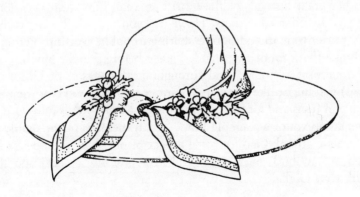

everyone has their favourite vegetables (today is not a day for forcing anyone to eat spinach 'because it's good for them'!). Make the dessert a once-a-year treat (the Paradise torte described in the previous chapter has become our traditional Easter dessert).

Easter Sunday afternoon is a good time for a family walk in the countryside (weather permitting). Why not make searching for new life a theme of the walk? Children can be encouraged to look for signs of new plants growing or birds building nests.

Activities for Easter Sunday

After the meal is over you might like to indulge in party games. The Christian community we used to live in runs a community 'Olympic Games' on Easter Sunday afternoon. This consists of a series of silly games suitable for all ages. Why not put together a selection of your favourite family games? Here are a couple which incorporate an Easter theme:

- *Egg rolling*: This is a traditional Easter Sunday pastime. All it requires is a hill and a selection of hard-boiled eggs. If there is no convenient hillside you could use an inclined plank of wood instead. The winner is the person whose egg remains uncracked longest. This game apparently originated as a symbol that the stone had been rolled away from Jesus' tomb.

- *Hunt the Easter egg*: This is a favourite with our children. We hide small foil-covered chocolate eggs around the house and garden. The search can keep them occupied for some time!

Prayers for Easter Sunday

We have deliberately not created a family liturgy for Easter Sunday. Like the other great festivals of the Christian year, this is an occasion best shared with other Christians. However, you may well want to have a family prayer time in addition to sharing in public worship. Perhaps this could take the form of an extended grace before Sunday lunch.

In your prayers today (and throughout the season of Easter which follows) you might like to make a point of thanking God for the new life we have in Jesus and for the new life we see all around us in nature. Why not make up your own simple litany? Each member of the family could take turns to thank God for some aspect of new life (the flowers in the garden, a new bird's nest, etc.) and everyone else could respond with 'Thank you, God'.

• *Paschal candle*: In some Christian traditions it is customary to light a special candle on Easter Sunday. This Paschal candle is used in worship until Ascension Day (or, in some cases, Pentecost). Its light is a powerful symbol of Jesus Christ's resurrection triumph over darkness and sin. Why not light a candle as part of your family prayers today? Let it remind you that the light of Christ has triumphed over darkness.

EASTERTIDE

Easter does not end with Easter Sunday. On the contrary, joyous as it is, Easter Sunday originally simply marked the beginning of fifty days of celebration culminating in Pentecost.

The first Eastertide was not just a period of celebration. The disciples certainly rejoiced that Jesus had returned to them from the dead. But it was also a time of preparation (an aspect which becomes clear in the New Testament accounts of the Ascension and the remaining days until Pentecost). Thus it is a season of celebration with a sense of direction. As we rejoice in the implications of the resurrection, we also prepare ourselves for its greatest implication: the coming of the Holy Spirit to enliven and empower the Church, individually and collectively.

Sadly the tradition of making this entire period a time of celebration to balance Lent has all but disappeared. However, we can begin to restore the note of joy and celebration that is appropriate to this season without resorting to an elaborate set of artificial new 'traditions'.

Family prayers during Eastertide

It is worth putting a little extra effort into maintaining the keynote of praise and celebration in our family prayers throughout the period from Easter Sunday to Pentecost. To begin with, we could make a point of using 'Alleluia' as a response, letting it become a verbal reminder that praise is the watchword of this entire season.

Setting: You could decorate the area you generally use for family prayers to reflect the note of joy and praise. Why not find some suitable flowers? A banner on the wall could portray Christian symbols relevant to the season. If you made or bought a family Paschal candle, this could be lit while you worship together.

Songs: Your favourite Easter hymns and choruses are appropriate
             throughout Eastertide. If you use songs in your family
             prayers, why not include some of these in your selection?

Themes: Why not pick an appropriate theme for family prayers
             during Eastertide? The Sunday themes in the Church of
             England's Alternative Service Book suggest the resur-
             rection appearances or the 'I am' sayings from John's
             Gospel.

Easter decorations

Our homes and our churches could reflect more clearly the joy of
Eastertide. For example, we could begin to build up collections of Easter
decorations in much the same way as most households possess boxes of
Christmas decorations. In our home we keep the Easter cards we have
received on display until Pentecost. Colourful banners and wall-hangings,
'stained glass' pictures in our windows, seasonal flowers, Easter symbols;
all these could be used to create an atmosphere of celebration.

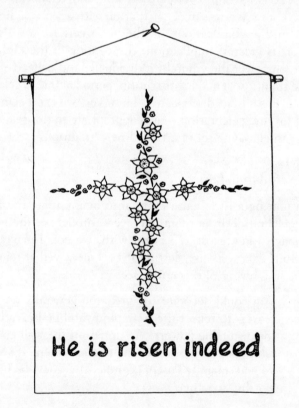

Hospitality

Hospitality is an important aspect of this atmosphere. As we noted in the previous chapter, it was traditional for friends and families to get together for celebrations after Easter. This practice could be extended throughout Eastertide. For example, each weekend we might invite one or two friends, neighbours, or church members to join us for a meal. Conversely we could make an extra effort to visit those who cannot come to us. We need to take time to share with others our joy at Christ's resurrection.

Since the dining table (rather than the television) is the traditional heart of the home this could be decorated to reflect our festive mood. Why not invest in or make a special brightly coloured tablecloth? If you don't have a special prayer corner, the family Paschal candle could be the centrepiece, lit whenever you eat together.

Activities for Eastertide

Here are a few suggestions which reflect the theme of new life.

• *Caterpillars and butterflies*: You can easily make caterpillars out of old egg boxes. Cut the carton into strips and let the children stick cotton wool on to make them fuzzy. Pipe cleaners make good antennae.

Old-fashioned wooden clothes pegs can be used as the body of a butterfly. Insert a large square of coloured tissue paper into the peg and gather firmly to make the wings. Wrap a pipe cleaner round the head of the peg to make the antennae.

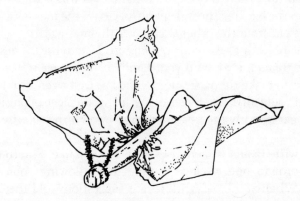

- *Planting seeds*: None of the members of our family are accomplished gardeners, so we have to use seeds that are easy to grow and germinate quickly. Bean sprouts, mustard or cress are all very easy to grow and have the added advantage that they can be eaten. Alternatively, you might like to have a go at growing something more ornamental (a number of annuals, including some antirrhinum, coleus, petunia and schizanthus, can be grown as pot plants).

  Planting seeds together is a good opportunity to talk about how new life can spring from a seed that looks dead and dry. You might like to refer to the way in which Jesus used the image of a seed sown in the ground to describe his own death and resurrection (John 12.24).

- *Easter nests*: These are simply made from cornflakes bound together by a coating of melted chocolate. In our family we make them throughout the year, but at Easter they become little nests in which we place small chocolate eggs. Even young children will enjoy helping to make them.

The tree of life

This idea for an Eastertide activity board was inspired partly by some suggestions of Joan Halmo[1] and partly by the medieval image of the cross as the tree of life.

You will need two large sheets of white cardboard: one for the tree, the other for the backing. Draw or paint a large cross entwined by seven flowering vines on one of the sheets. Six of your vines should have seven flowers each and the seventh should have eight, giving you fifty in all. The flowers should each be large enough to hide a simple message. When the paint is dry cut part of the way round each flower to form a flap. Mount this sheet on the other. (A simpler variation on this is to draw the cross and vines on the backing sheet, leaving spaces for the messages. Then blu-tack flowers cut from the other sheet over the messages.)

Now you are ready to write in your Eastertide activities. These could be little secret treats for you and your family to enjoy each day. Use your imagination to make the suggestions varied as well as enjoyable. Perhaps one day you could all dance together to a favourite piece of music; or make biscuits; or get up early the next morning to watch the sun rise; or go out for a walk.

You can write in all fifty activities at once if you like. Alternatively you may prefer to do one week at a time thus allowing yourself greater flexibility. When you have written your suggestions fold the flaps down carefully to hide them.

The flowers can be dated so that you work through the items as with an Advent calendar. If you prefer a little more mystery, leave them undated and allow family members who do not know what message is underneath to pick a flower each day. Of course, if you choose the latter course, you should make sure that the surprises are not too dependent on the weather, require elaborate preparation, or can only take place on a certain date!

SPECIAL OCCASIONS DURING EASTERTIDE

Easter Monday

This is not part of the liturgical structure of Easter, but it is a fact of life in the UK. We have a Bank Holiday which we can use to continue the celebrations of Easter Sunday. By letting our celebrations spill over on to the Monday, we underline the fact that Easter is not an isolated annual celebration. On the contrary, its effects spill over into the whole year just as the effects of the first Easter affect the whole of life.

We sometimes take our children to a local turkey farm on Easter Monday. There, as well as looking at a variety of other animals, they are able to watch chicks hatching.

Ascension Day

The fortieth day of Eastertide marks an essential stage in Jesus' preparation of the disciples for their larger mission. This is the day on which we recall Jesus' ascension. With the ascension his redemptive work reached its climax. The Greek Fathers of the Church used to say 'God became man that man might become God.' The ascension is the fulfilment of the incarnation. The second Person of the Trinity did not become a human being temporarily. On the contrary, the whole point of the ascension is to underline that God in his grace has made human nature a permanent part of the divine nature.

The ascension story suggests two major themes which offer fruitful starting points for family activities today: Jesus' kingship and his departure.

- *King Jesus*: Jesus ascended to take his place as King of the World. We can stress the theme of kingship and authority in a variety of ways:
  - ☐ make and wear paper crowns

☐ have the children dress up as kings or queens and act out their understanding of kingship

☐ watch a video which highlights the theme (e.g. an episode from the TV series *Elizabeth R*)

☐ listen to an appropriate piece of music (e.g. Handel's *Music for the Royal Fireworks*).

Having thus replayed the everyday understanding of kingship and authority, we can contrast it with the kind of king Jesus was and is (e.g. by comparing it with Jesus' own teaching on authority in Mark 10.35–45).

• *Partings*: Another aspect of Jesus' ascension is his departure. He was saying goodbye to his disciples. However, he was leaving for a reason. Without his departure there would have been no Pentecost. Thus, when tackling this theme, the aim is to stress that the immediate sorrow of separation may open the way to greater fulfilment in the future.

Why not have a family discussion about partings? You could talk about your experiences of separation. How do we remember people (memories, stories, photographs, etc.)? How do we keep in touch?

• *Countdown to Pentecost*: Ascension gives fresh impetus to our preparations. We begin counting the days to Pentecost. A Pentecost calendar, modelled on the traditional Advent calendar, is one way in which this may be done. Nine days from Ascension Day to Pentecost: perhaps our calendar could consist of nine empty rectangles drawn on a large sheet of paper. As each day arrives one of the rectangles could be filled in with a picture (possibly symbols representing the Holy Spirit and the gifts and fruits of the Spirit). The images which we add to the calendar day by day can become the focal point for family prayers as Pentecost approaches.

• *Flowers for Ascension*: One traditional name for the horse chestnut is the Ascension Tree, probably because it is in bloom at this time of year. Why not use its candle-like clusters of flowers in an arrangement for Ascension? You could also use flowering cherry or almond, white spiraea, white allium. Variegated ivy could be used for the background foliage.

Setting: Perhaps today's prayers could be held out of doors. Why not take the family to climb the nearest hill?

Reading: The story of the ascension can be found in Luke 24.50–53.

Songs: 'Hail the day that sees him rise' (AMNS 87, MP 202)

'Jesus shall reign' (AMNS 143, MP 379, SOF 301)
'The head that once was crowned with thorns' (AMNS 141, MP 647, SOF 531)

Prayer: 'Lord, the story of your ascension reminds us that you rule over all things. Help us to trust you in every aspect of our family life, especially when we are faced with difficulties and uncertainties. Grant that we may know your will and help us to glorify you by obeying it at all times. Amen.'

St George's Day (23rd April)

Little is known of the Christian martyr who inspired the legends of St George. But because he symbolized the ideal of the Christian knight, he became very popular in the Middle Ages and was adopted as the patron saint of soldiers. Edward III made him patron of the Order of the Garter and subsequently he was adopted as the patron saint of England. Amongst other places to adopt him as their patron are Portugal, Catalonia and Genoa.

The legend of George slaying the dragon first appears in the twelfth century. A good modern retelling of the legend for children (of all ages) is *A Bad Year for Dragons* (Bodley Head, 1986) by John Ryan, the creator of Captain Pugwash. This legend could have been made for acting out: why not encourage the younger members of the family to turn it into a play? This could well be the starting point for a discussion about the 'dragons' we have to face today (e.g. bullying, drugs, racism, violence, pollution).

Since George is the patron saint of England, this is a good day for remembering some of the good things about England. Why not have a traditional English dinner? Elgar's *Pomp and Circumstance Marches* (source of the tune for 'Land of Hope and Glory') could provide a very English musical accompaniment.

- *A St George's Day shield*: Making a shield to celebrate St George is a simple activity for any children in your family. Simply provide each of them with a large sheet of card and a set of felt-tipped pens. Ask them to design a suitable emblem for the shield perhaps using St George's Cross (a red cross on a white background), a dragon or a rose.

Reading: Eph. 6.10–18 (the armour of God)
Songs: 'A safe stronghold our God is still' (AMNS 114, MP 2, SOF 25)
             'Rejoice!' (MP 572, SOF 480)
             'Soldiers of Christ, arise' (AMNS 219, MP 604, SOF 506)
             'We rest on thee' (MP 735, SOF 587)
Prayers: Since George is patron of England, this nation is an appropriate theme for family prayers today: listen to the news and pick out two or three specific issues about which to pray. Another possibility would be to pray for those who defend the weak against the strong and those who seek to combat the dragons of our time.

St Mark's Day (25th April)

John Mark was the cousin of Barnabas who accompanied Paul and Barnabas on their first missionary journey. Subsequently he joined Barnabas on a missionary journey to Cyprus (Acts 15.39) and still later was associated with both Paul (Col. 4.10) and Peter (1 Pet. 5.13) in Rome. Tradition has it that he was Peter's interpreter and, as such, wrote the Gospel which bears his name.

Reading: Mark 13.5–13
Songs: 'Tell out my soul' (MP 631, SOF 52)
             'We have a gospel to proclaim' (MP 728, AMNS 431)
Prayer: 'Lord, we give you thanks for the light cast by the witness of your evangelist St Mark. Enable us to be faithful to the teaching of the gospel both in word and deed. For your name's sake. Amen.'

7

Summer Festivals

PENTECOST

Once again we come to a central festival in the Church's year. This festival marks the end of Eastertide and the beginning of 'ordinary time'. Today we celebrate God's sending of the Holy Spirit in power to bring the Church into existence and maintain it in being.

Pentecost means the fiftieth day. In Jewish tradition it was a harvest festival. They celebrated the barley harvest on the day after the Sabbath following the Passover. Fifty days later, on Pentecost (or 'Shavuot'), they celebrated the wheat harvest. But it took on another, deeper, significance in Jewish tradition: it came to be associated with the giving of the Law to Moses on Mount Sinai.

For Christians, the first Pentecost took place fifty days after the resurrection of Jesus, when the disciples went to the Temple to celebrate Shavuot with their fellow Jews. In the midst of readings about the giving of the Law, the Spirit settled in power upon the disciples.

Songs: 'Breathe on me, breath of God' (AMNS 157, MP 67, SOF 51)
'Come down, O Love divine' (AMNS 156, MP 89)
'For I'm building a people of power' (JP 47, MP 151, SOF 111)
'O breath of life, come sweeping through us' (MP 488, SOF 407)
'Spirit of the living God' (JP 222, MP 613, SOF 510)
'Wind, wind, blow on me' (MP 771, SOF 609)

Readings: The story of Pentecost is to be found in Acts 2. Suitable Old Testament readings for the day include those which would be read in the synagogue to mark Shavuot: Exod. 19.1—20.17; Num. 28.26–31; Deut. 5.19–20, 9.9–19, 10.1–5,10; Ezek. 1.1–28, 3.12; Deut. 15.19—16.17; Hab. 2.20—3.19; Ruth.

Prayer: 'Lord, set our souls on fire with love, faith and hope by the
               power of your Holy Spirit. And may the wind of your Spirit
               so inspire us that we may share your good news with others
               in words that they can understand. Amen.'

The wind of the Spirit

Even more than many other Christian concepts, the idea of spirit is
difficult to get across to young children. However, by exploring air or
breath in some way we can deepen their understanding of something
which is the chief biblical metaphor for spirit. In this way we will be laying
solid foundations for future teaching.

For this reason we think flying a kite is an excellent way of spending the
afternoon at Pentecost. What better way to introduce children to the
power of the wind? We have a very simple inexpensive kite made from
nylon and glassfibre. It flies well even in light winds and is easy enough for
a five-year-old to control.

Other ways of illustrating the power of invisible air include sailing boats, balloons, windmills (real and toy), musical instruments (recorders, whistles, harmonicas), blowing bubbles, flags waving, and clouds.

Young children may not have associated air with breath. Try asking them to watch you breathe. Tell them that we need air to live. Get them to blow on their hands so that they can feel the air that helps them to live.

Kitemaking

If you don't possess a kite, you can make your own. Look in your local library for books on kitemaking. These will give you details of how to construct kites of almost any degree of complexity.

If you have very young children and want to keep things simple, you can make a 'kite' from a polystyrene tile. Simply tape a paper tail to one corner and a length of thread to the underside of the tile. It doesn't really fly but it is so light that it will stay aloft as long as the child is running! If you like, you or the child could decorate this 'kite' with felt-tipped pen.

A simple windmill

You can make a very effective windmill from a square of paper, a pin and a short garden cane.

1. Draw diagonals on the paper square and then draw a small circle around the centre of the square where they intersect.
2. Cut along each of the four lines from the corner to the edge of the circle.
3. You should now have four triangles of paper joined at the centre. Using the pin, make a hole in the right hand corner of each triangle.
4. Push the pin through one of the holes from underneath. Fold over the next corner and push the pin through that. Continue until all the corners are bent over. Finally push the pin through the centre of the square.
5. Pin the folded square to the cane to complete your windmill.

Poems about the wind

> 'The Wind' (Robert Louis Stevenson)
> 'Wind' (Ted Hughes)
> 'The West Wind' (John Masefield)
> 'The Wind' (Emily Dickinson)
> 'Night Wind' (John Clare)
> 'The wind was on the withered heath' (J. R. R. Tolkien from *The Hobbit*)
> 'And it was windy weather' (James Stephens)
> 'The Wind' (Christina Rossetti)
> 'Windy Nights' (Robert Louis Stevenson)

A birthday party for your church

Pentecost is the Church's birthday. It is a good excuse for an extra birthday party! Ideally this is something which could be organized by the Church itself (perhaps by the Sunday School or Youth Group).

- *Flower arrangements*: The themes of wind and fire offer plenty of potential for imaginative flower arrangements. Predominantly red flowers (e.g. gerbera, tulip) could represent fire. Look out for other colours: orange, gold, yellow. You could use ornamental grasses to create an impression of wind.

- *Food*: Since we are celebrating the coming of the Holy Spirit to give birth to the Church you could make a cake in the shape of a dove. It is traditional in Jewish homes to celebrate Shavuot with dairy foods. Apparently this is to recall the Promised Land, flowing with milk and honey. Why not celebrate the coming of the Spirit with all those high cholesterol foods we are so careful to avoid nowadays?

- *Cheese blintzes*: These are delicious, simple to make, and a traditional part of Shavuot/Pentecost celebrations.
  Start by making pancakes (see p. 64), but instead of tossing them, allow them to cook on one side until the top is dry then remove from the pan. Place them brown side up and put a tablespoon of cream cheese on top (perhaps mixed with some sugar and cinnamon). Fold the sides in and roll up like a sausage roll. Now fry these packages to brown the uncooked outside.

TRINITY SUNDAY

The Sunday after Pentecost is widely celebrated as Trinity Sunday: the day on which we focus upon *who* our God is: Father, Son *and* Holy Spirit, three Persons but one God. Christians today often shy away from the idea of the Trinity because it seems too difficult. It *is* difficult to explain but the reason for this difficulty is that God as Trinity is fundamental to Christian faith. The mistake lies in trying to explain something that is fundamental. Physicists have the same difficulty when they are asked to explain what mass is: it cannot be explained because it is one of the fundamentals used to explain everything else. The same is true of Christianity: we cannot explain the Trinity, but the rest of orthodox Christian belief only fully makes sense if we are talking about *this* God.

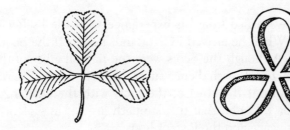

We cannot explain the Trinity. But we can and should celebrate the fact that this is our God.

Visual images:	Some years ago, while visiting Israel, Diana was given a large reproduction of Andrei Rublev's *Icon of the Holy Trinity* which we use as a centrepiece for our prayer corner on Trinity Sunday.
	If you feel uncomfortable with an icon, why not make a simple flower arrangement using three flowers and/or three branches arranged to express the idea of three making up a single whole? You could use contorted willow twigs or broom, tulips or gerberas. Another possibility would be to use some shamrock or the paper shamrocks from St Patrick's Day.
Reading:	John 14.8–17
Songs:	'Father, Lord of all creation' (AMNS 356)
	'Father, we adore you' (JP 44, MP 139, SOF 99)

'Father, we love you' (JP 45, MP 142, SOF 102)

'Holy, Holy, Holy' (AMNS 95, MP 237, SOF 183)

Prayer: 'The Father is my hope; the Son is my refuge; the Holy Spirit is my protector. O All-holy Trinity, glory to thee. Amen.'

(*A Greek Orthodox prayer to the Holy Trinity*)

ST COLUMBA (9th June)

Columba was a rather belligerent Irishman. Indeed, according to legend, he started a war over a copy of a Psalter! Three thousand men were killed in that war and Columba was exiled from Ireland. Thus, at the age of 40, he arrived on the Island of Iona and began the work of bringing the gospel to the Picts.

One thing he learned from his experience with the Psalter was the futility of war. When he arrived in Scotland, he found the Scots at war with the Picts. Although the Scots were the natural allies of the Irish, Columba refused to side with them against the Picts. Instead he walked to Inverness to confront the chief of the Picts with the challenge of the gospel. Columba told him that true strength lay not in violence but in facing life with peace and the love of Jesus.

In time Iona became a great monastery, the spiritual heart of Scotland and a centre of peace. The warlike Columba eventually lived up to his name which means 'dove': the symbol of peace.

Reading: Matt. 5.43–48

Songs: 'Eternal Ruler of the ceaseless round' (AMNS 353)

'Make me a channel of your peace' (JP 161, MP 456, SOF 381)

'Peace I give to you' (JP 196, MP 554)

'Peace is flowing like a river' (MP 555, SOF 458)

Prayers: Making peace the focus of family prayers seems very appropriate for a day on which we remember such a person. Perhaps you could listen together to the news and pray particularly for one troublespot. Why not find a picture of a dove and use it as the focal point for your prayers?

'Peace between neighbours,
Peace between kindred,
Peace between lovers,
In love of the King of life.

Peace between person and person,
Peace between wife and husband,
Peace between woman and children,
The peace of Christ above all peace.'
(*A Gaelic prayer for peace*)

ST JOHN THE BAPTIST (24th June)

This is reckoned to be the birthday of St John the Baptist since, according to Luke, he was born three months after the Annunciation (25th March). A midsummer celebration is doubly appropriate since John himself said, 'He must increase, but I must decrease': after midsummer the days start getting shorter again.

You may feel that this is an appropriate day to think about baptisms or to engage in activities involving water. Why not use it as an excuse for a family swim?

Since the feast coincides with midsummer, it is worth exploring some of the midsummer traditions which have been linked to the festival. For example, in pre-Christian times it was customary to light a bonfire at midsummer. The practice continued and the fires came to be known as St John's fires (particularly appropriate as St John's Gospel refers to John the Baptist as a witness to the light).

Reading: Matt. 3 or John 1.19–34
Songs: 'On Jordan's bank the Baptist's cry' (AMNS 27, MP 538)
Prayer: 'Lord, we thank you for the example of John. Help us to be truthful and bold as we share your good news with others. Amen.'

ST PETER (29th June)

This is the day on which many churches celebrate Simon Peter ('the Rock'), a simple Galilean fisherman who became the leader of the Christian community after Pentecost. In many churches it is also a favourite day for ordaining people to the Christian ministry.

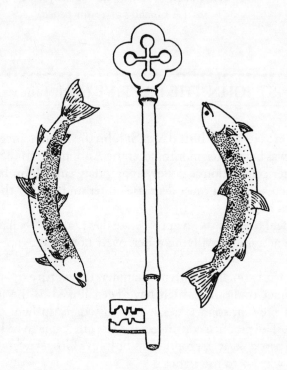

Simon Peter is a very human character. A man of great faith, he was nevertheless capable of making mistakes and letting others down.

Pebble painting

Why not paint symbols of St Peter (fish, fishing net, keys or ship) on a smooth pebble? Once the paint has dried the pebbles can be varnished to protect the picture.

The pebble picks up the theme of Peter the Rock. You could use it to talk about different properties of rock which might have led Jesus to use this nickname for Peter.

You could also tie this in with the theme of fishing and fishermen by taking a trip to the seaside in order to collect the pebbles.

Peter the fisherman

Peter's connection with fishing is a useful source of ideas for activities with younger children.

- *Fish collage*: Even very young children can cut simple fish shapes out of brightly coloured paper, and stick them on to a large background sheet.

- *Magnetic fishing*: Many parents will recognize this as a popular game for young children. It has been available for many years in various commercial guises, though it is very easy to make your own set. All that is required are some small garden canes, string and some small magnets. Suitable magnets can sometimes be obtained from commercial stationers or toyshops. If you have any difficulty in finding these, you could use sticky velcro pads instead. Tie the magnets to the canes to form fishing rods. Use the shapes cut out for the collage as fish and simply attach a small paper clip to the head of each one.

Family prayers for Petertide

If your denomination is one that ordains its ministers at Petertide, this would be a good topic for your prayers today. Find out who is being ordained in your area and pray for them and their situation by name.

FAMILY HOLIDAYS

The annual holiday has become a traditional part of modern life. A generation ago the summer months would have seen a mass exodus from the cities to seaside resorts like Blackpool, Brighton and Bognor. Today we migrate in flocks to the sunnier beaches of Majorca or the Costa del Sol. We seek a break from the routine, new experiences, a completely different way of life (if only for a week or ten days).

Many Christian parents will want to continue family prayers during the holidays. On the other hand, they will not want to make a chore out of it. The whole point of the holiday is to escape from the chores and the routine. For this reason we are limiting our suggestions to one or two ideas intended to maximize our enjoyment of the holiday.

A *holiday journal*

If, like us, you tend to holiday in the British Isles, you will be familiar with the problem of rainy days. These are a particular problem if you have several children in tow. Unless you have something to occupy them, they easily degenerate into a cycle of 'I'm bored . . .', 'What can we do now?', 'He hit me first . . .'

We encourage our children to keep a holiday journal. It requires only minimal preparation before the holiday and is capable of keeping our children (more or less) quiet for up to an hour every time we are faced with a rainy day.

Preparation amounts to remembering to pack a scrapbook (or ring binder and paper), pencils and/or pens, a glue stick, ruler, eraser and scissors. On days out during the holiday itself we make a point of visiting local tourist information centres and collecting all the free brochures and maps that are available: these provide much of the raw material for the journal.

The idea of the journal is to create an illustrated record of the holiday. This can include brochures, postcards, maps, tickets, stamps, paintings, drawings, recollections: whatever will help the child remember a particular day of the holidays. It is not a chore or an exercise and should not be forced on children. But if they can be persuaded to keep a journal, it provides them with a permanent record of what they did and thus extends their enjoyment of the holiday into the following months and years.

There are many different ways of praying: keeping a journal has often been seen by Christians as one form. Why not share this idea with the members of your family? Discuss who they might write the journal for. A journal addressed to God is a written prayer.

A holiday theme or project

Some people are content to lie on a beach for a fortnight while the children build endless sandcastles (or, more likely, demand money for the latest amusement arcade). Judging by the growth in thematic holidays many others find that boring and prefer something more purposeful.

One way of injecting a sense of purpose into a holiday is to choose a theme for the holiday. This is simply a matter of agreeing to focus on some aspect of the holiday area: its history, archaeology, natural history, culture or whatever else strikes you as particularly interesting.

Don't overlook the possibility that there may be themes relevant to the faith of your family which can be explored on holiday. How did Christianity come to the place you will be visiting? Are there any sites of particular Christian significance? Why not link up with the Christians who live there now? A visit to a welcoming church in a strange place can be a very powerful reminder that the Church is a family which transcends all the usual boundaries.

Preparation may amount to a visit or two to your local library to obtain any necessary background information. There may be things you need to pack (field guides, binoculars, etc.). The point is not to turn the holiday into work but rather to enable you to encounter the place and the people you are visiting more fully. Such encounters create shared memories which may last a lifetime. They may lead to friendships which will enrich your family life in years to come. They may provide us with fresh ideas for family celebrations and they certainly serve to strengthen our sense of being a family.

Family prayers on holiday

Different families will take different views on what to do about family prayers on holidays. Some will feel it is important to carry on as usual. Others will want to emphasize the break in routine by dropping the routine of family prayers.

We personally tend to the 'business as usual' end of the spectrum. However, there is a lot to be said for doing something different. You may well have to change the time or the structure of family prayers because of the nature of your holiday. If you are camping or flying to your holiday destination, you may want to keep books to a minimum. If the hotel serves dinner just when you normally say prayers, you will have to rearrange your schedule.

Since it is a scheduled break in your usual routine, this could be a good opportunity to experiment with a different pattern of prayers. If you normally read from the Bible, why not take some other suitable book instead? If you use set prayers, why not leave your prayer book at home and experiment with extempore prayers? Why not pack a candle and experiment with silent prayer? Yet another possibility would be to look out for churches while you are on holiday and spend a few minutes praying silently in one of the local churches each day.

Prayers for a journey

Blessed are you, Lord of those who travel and those who stay at home. You created a wonderful world in which we can travel.
We ask you to be with us as we prepare to leave on our journey of rest and relaxation.
Keep us free from harm and evil on the road.
Help us to see more clearly the beauty of your creation as we travel, and help us to appreciate each other more fully in the days that lie ahead.
Bless us as we set off, and bring us safely home again. Amen.

> Alone with none but thee, my God,
> I journey on my way.
> What need I fear, when thou art near,
> O King of night and day?
> More safe am I within thy hand
> Than if a host did round me stand.
> (*St Columba*)

Thank you, Lord, for all the fun of travelling. Thank you for interesting vehicles and exciting new places to see. Watch over us and all who travel today, and bring us safely to our destination.

Prayer for holidays

Dear God, thank you for our holidays: for sunshine and fresh air, for countryside and beaches. Help us to appreciate the beauty of your creation and make new friends as we enjoy ourselves today.

THE FEAST OF THE TRANSFIGURATION (6th August)

This festival recalls the incident in the Gospels when Jesus was transfigured on a mountain top. As Mark tells the story (Mark 9.2–9), it was a crucial point in Jesus' earthly ministry. The Law (represented by Moses), the prophets (represented by Elijah) and the voice of God himself all testify to the fact that Jesus is God's Son. Immediately after this anticipation of his eventual glorification, he set out upon the road to Jerusalem and death.

Since the end of the Second World War it has had another meaning in many minds. 6th August was the day on which the Allies dropped an atomic bomb on the Japanese city of Hiroshima. For that reason, the Feast of the Transfiguration is also known as Peace Day: a day on which people all over the world recall the horrors of war and pray for peace.

There is a very moving children's book which tells the story of Sadako Sasaki, a girl who died of leukaemia as a result of the Hiroshima bomb. Written by Eleanor Coerr, it is called *Sadako and the Thousand Paper Cranes* (Hodder & Stoughton, 1981). Why not read the story together as a family? Today a statue of Sadako stands in Hiroshima's Peace Park. On it is engraved the following prayer:

> This is our cry,
> this is our prayer;
> peace in the world.

ST AIDAN (31st August)

Aidan of Lindisfarne is one of the great figures of the history of Christianity in the British Isles. Educated on Iona, he was responsible for bringing the good news of Jesus Christ to many people in Northumbria. The monastery he founded at Lindisfarne became one of the great centres of Christianity in northern Europe.

A prayer walk

Aidan maintained a very simple lifestyle, walking everywhere rather than riding. Indeed when King Oswin gave him a horse, he soon gave it away. The Celtic spirituality which he imbibed at Iona puts great emphasis on the presence of God in nature and everyday life. As he walked, Aidan greeted everyone he met and shared the good news with them. Doubtless he also prayed to the God who was with him on the road.

A prayer walk is one way of recapturing that sense of God's presence in the everyday. It may be in the countryside or in the town. Wherever you choose to walk, the point is to pray about the things and people you encounter on your walk. The suggestions that follow were written with a country walk in mind but may easily be adapted for use in an urban or suburban setting.

Begin by taking a few moments to relax and become aware of God's presence and his love for you. As you step outside, breathe deeply . . . reflect on how you take the air you breathe for granted. Think about the other necessities of life which God provides.

When you have walked far enough to be out of earshot of anyone, pause and make conscious prayerful use of each one of your senses in turn.

Sight
Use your vision to revel in, enjoy, discern the colour, shape, texture, depth, movement of everything around you. Think about what the beauty in all around you contributes to your life. Consider the privilege and responsibility which God has given you in the gift of all this beauty. Express to God your thanksgiving and praise.

Hearing
Stop for a while and really listen, listen to the silence which, in reality, is teeming with natural sounds. Listen for the breeze blowing through the trees or through the long grass; listen for the song of birds, and for the hum of insects. Imagine the wind, the trees, the insects and the birds all blending their voices together in a song of praise to their Creator. Add your voice to their worship.

Touch
Become conscious of the feeling of the sun and the air on your skin, the textures of clothing, trees, grass, stones, the sensation of the ground through your shoes.

If you have time, you might like to do the same with your senses of taste and smell.

Conclude by finding one thing which summarizes for you what you have experienced during this walk.

ST MATTHEW (21st September)

Tradition has it that St Matthew was the author of the first of the Gospels, but we are actually told very little about Matthew in the New Testament. He appears in all the lists of the apostles (Matt. 10.3, Mark 3.18, Luke 6.15, Acts 1.13) and is described as a tax collector (Matt. 9.9, 10.3) but that is all.

Even this minimal description provides us with an important theme which may be used for family prayers today. Tax collectors were among the most hated people in Jesus' day. They worked for the Romans, who had enslaved the Jewish people. Even worse, they often grew rich by cheating and stealing, demanding even more tax money than the Romans required and keeping the extra for themselves. And yet it was just such a person to whom Jesus said 'Follow me!'

Why not read or act the story of another biblical tax collector, Zacchaeus (Luke 19.1–10)? Talk about people who are hated today. What difference does it make that Jesus can say to them 'Follow me'?

Zacchaeus had been selfish and grasping. His meeting with Jesus transformed him into someone who was generous with his wealth. This may be a good cue to think about your giving as a family. In the light of Zacchaeus' generosity, what proportion of your money do you think it would be appropriate to give? Or do you have time or special skills that you can give to others instead?

8

Michaelmas and Autumn

ST MICHAEL AND ALL ANGELS (29th September)

Some readers may wonder why we should want to celebrate angels. Are they not merely a slightly embarrassing hangover from a pre-modern era when people still believed in elves, fairies and all manner of supernatural beings?

A couple of decades ago it might well have been possible to dismiss angels in that way. However, we appear to have entered a period of significant cultural change. The scientifically informed materialism and scepticism of a generation ago no longer satisfies. Millions of people in the western world are desperately exploring the spiritual dimensions of human experience in the hope of finding something more meaningful than materialism. Books about angels now regularly feature in the non-fiction bestsellers' lists. Sadly these books are often ill-informed as to the significance of angels in Christian belief.

The Bible presents angels as ministering spirits: the agents and messengers of God. They bring into personal focus the multitude of ways in which God speaks to us through his creation. As spirits they are the inhabitants of the invisible spiritual depths of creation.

They turn up at key points in Jesus' life and ministry, announcing his incarnation (Luke 1.26–38) and birth (Luke 2.9–15), assisting him in the wilderness (Matt. 4.11), comforting him in Gethsemane (Luke 22.43) and present at his resurrection (Matt. 28.2–7). Subsequently, they appear in Acts, giving assistance to the first Christians at crucial moments.

Given their importance in Christian teaching and the resurgence of popular interest in spiritual beings, it is entirely appropriate to pay attention to angels in family worship.

Michaelmas activities

● *Angel paper-chains*: Cut a long strip from a large sheet of paper and concertina it into four (or six) segments. Draw an angel outline on the paper, making sure that its wingtips are part of the fold. Cut and unfold it to reveal a chain of figures. These can be coloured in by the children and hung up as decorations for your Michaelmas celebrations.

- *Books for Michaelmas*: Angels feature in a number of books by the award-winning children's writer Madeleine l'Engle. Her best known book is *A Wrinkle in Time* (Puffin, 1967) (in which the angels take the unlikely form of Mrs Whatsit, Mrs Who and Mrs Which). If you enjoy that, you might try its sequels: *A Wind in the Door* (Dell Publishing, 1976), *A Swiftly Tilting Planet* (Dell Publishing, 1979) and *Many Waters* (Hodder & Stoughton, 1992).

- *Angels in art*: Angels appear frequently in western art. Why not explore the art books at your local library to see what you can find? Look particularly for paintings of the events in Jesus' life mentioned above.
  One of the most dramatic examples in recent art is Epstein's stark and unsentimental sculpture of St Michael slaying the dragon (Rev. 12.7–9) which is on display at Coventry Cathedral.

Songs:	'All heaven declares' (MP 14, SOF 10)
	'Angel-voices, ever singing' (AMNS 163, MP 34, SOF 24)
	'Come, let us join our cheerful songs' (AMNS 144, MP 93, SOF 70)
	'Praise, my soul' (AMNS 192, JP 204, MP 560, SOF 466)
	'Ye holy angels bright' (AMNS 198, MP 783, SOF 619)
Readings:	Ps. 150; Dan. 7.9–14, 9.20–23; Rev. 5, 12.7–12a

Prayer: 'Father God,
            we stand in awe before your creation with its marvellous
            interweaving of matter and spirit:
            grant that as your holy angels always serve you in heaven,
            so, at your command, they may help and defend us on
            earth; through Jesus Christ our Lord. Amen.'

HARVEST THANKSGIVING

Modern life has largely insulated us from the natural world. Our
technology protects us from many natural dangers but, at the same time,
isolates us from nature. Living and working in an urban environment we
easily become unconscious of the changing seasons. Even our food is
prepackaged to such an extent that it is easy to lose sight of its natural
origins.

For such reasons, charges of irrelevance are sometimes laid against church harvest festivals. Does it really make any sense to deck a suburban church with wheat sheafs? What are we to make of a congregation of stockbrokers or shipbuilders singing 'We plough the fields and scatter'? What meaning can harvest have for people who have come no closer to picking their own food than removing tins from the supermarket shelves?

And yet, the global environmental crisis facing humankind at the end of the twentieth century is a mute reminder of the perils of ignoring the natural world. Our culture has encouraged us to think of nature as something out there: a source of raw materials, a bottomless sink for our waste, something to be enjoyed in small doses on holiday. We need, as a matter of urgency, to rediscover our intimate interconnectedness with the natural world. Far from being 'out there' somewhere, we are embedded in it.

Harvest thanksgiving may seem quaint and irrelevant as we approach a new millenium. In fact, it is one way in which we can remind ourselves and our children that we are utterly dependent upon God's good creation for our continued existence. When we give thanks for the harvest, we acknowledge our dependence upon God for life. But we also acknowledge that his way of sustaining our lives is through natural processes.

Harvest activities

Family activities for harvest-time might centre upon visits to places which remind us of our rootedness in nature. Why not visit a farm (of the traditional kind rather than a factory farm)? Many farms are now open to the public. Town and city dwellers need not feel excluded since there is a

growing number of town farms (often sponsored by town or city authorities to perform an educational function).

Even better, why not visit a 'pick your own' orchard or market garden? These are not just limited to strawberries and soft fruit. An increasing number offer a wide range of fruit and vegetables for customers to harvest. If you do not have your own vegetable patch, this is an ideal opportunity for you to experience the meaning of harvesting.

Alternatively why not visit a public park or botanic garden? When we lived in London, Kew and Wisley were favourites with our children, but every city offers chances to relax and observe the changing seasons.

If you can find a pile of leaves, why not indulge in a favourite child's pastime of previous generations: jumping in the leaf pile and kicking them around! Our culture encourages us to be spectators rather than participants. From time to time, we need to remind ourselves of the reality of nature by touching it. Of course, you should always put the pile back when you have finished playing. Otherwise, you may have an irate gardener after you!

A thanksgiving dinner

Harvest is a time for enjoying the fruit of the earth. Therefore a celebratory dinner is particularly appropriate.

Given what we have been saying about recalling our connections with the natural world, we would tend to avoid convenience foods for such a meal. Packaged high-tech meals obscure the natural (or unnatural) origins of their contents. Why not try to make as much use of seasonable produce as possible? If this includes fruit or vegetables which you have picked from your own garden or from a 'pick your own' business, so much the better. There is something very satisfying about eating what you have grown (or, at least, harvested) yourself.

Preferring fresh seasonal produce to frozen (or otherwise packaged) food means that more time will be required to prepare the meal. Why not make the preparation time part of the celebration by getting the whole family to participate as far as possible?

Celebrating creation in music

Beethoven	6th Symphony ('The Pastoral')
Bliss	The World is Charged with the Grandeur of God
Bruckner	4th Symphony
Copland	In the Beginning

Debussy	*Prélude à l'Après-Midi d'un Faune*
Haydn	*The Creation*
	The Seasons
Tavener	*Akathist of Thanksgiving*
Vivaldi	*The Four Seasons*
Runrig	'Amazing Things'
	'Our Earth Was Once Green'

Give thanks to God

Although strictly speaking it refers to the early summer thanksgiving festival of Pentecost, the Book of Ruth is an appropriate reading at harvest-time. Many of the Psalms refer to God's goodness in providing for our material needs (e.g. Pss. 65.9–13, 104, 136): these may be read as prayers or used as the basis for our own prayers.

O God, we thank you for this earth, our home; for the wide sky and the shining sun, for the salt sea and the running water, for the everlasting hills and the never-resting winds, for trees and the green grass underfoot. Grant us a heart wide open to all this beauty; and save our souls from being so blind that we pass unseeing when the thornbush is aflame with your glory.

Increase our sense of fellowship with all living things, our little brothers, to whom you have given this earth. We remember with shame how often we have exercised our dominion with ruthless cruelty. May we realize that they live, not for us alone, but for themselves and for you.

May we not leave anything ravished by our greed or spoiled by our ignorance, but may we hand on our common heritage fairer and sweeter through our use of it, undiminished in fertility and joy.

(adapted from Walter Rauschenbusch)

Why not find or write a litany of thanksgiving for the occasion? (A litany is a series of short prayers with a response repeated between them.)

Leader:	Lord, you have kept your gracious promise that while earth remains, seed-time and harvest shall not cease.
All:	We thank you, heavenly Father.
Leader:	For giving us the fruits of the earth in their seasons, to strengthen and make glad our hearts,

All:	We thank you, heavenly Father.
Leader:	For all who labour to bring us our daily food,
All:	We thank you, heavenly Father.
Leader:	For the wonder of nature and the beauty of the earth,
All:	We thank you, heavenly Father.

(adapted from Michael Botting)

A simple DIY litany, naming the contents of the harvest meal, might be an appropriate grace to say today.

Yet another possibility would be to sing an appropriate hymn or song as a prayer of thanksgiving. For example:

'For the beauty of the earth' (AMNS 104; JP 48; MP 152; SOF 112)

'For the fruits of his creation' (AMNS 457; MP 153)

'Now thank we all our God' (AMNS 206; MP 486; JP 175; SOF 405)

'Praise and thanksgiving' (AMNS 415)

'We plough the fields, and scatter' (AMNS 290, JP 267, MP 732, SOF 585).

ST FRANCIS (4th October)

Francis must be one of the best known and loved of all the saints. Many stories are told of him; stories which highlight his simplicity, generosity, humility, desire for peace and love of nature. The last of these characteristics seems particularly important to modern people with our awareness of how much damage we have done to the environment. Not surprisingly, he is widely regarded as the patron saint of ecology.

It seems very appropriate that his feast day should coincide with that time of year when we celebrate harvest thanksgiving. You might even like to use St Francis' Day as your family day for harvest thanksgiving. This is certainly a good day for celebrating the natural world and thanking God for the goodness of creation.

Creation-centred family activities

Why not visit a zoo or wildlife park today? We live near an animal sanctuary which is a favourite afternoon out for our children. Alterna-

tively, you might like to spend some time in the countryside. If so, here
are some activities to add to your enjoyment:

• *Mini-beast safari*: Each person will need a few feet of string and a
  magnifying glass. Lay your string across the most interesting piece of
  ground you can find to form your 'nature trail'. Crawl slowly along the
  length of the string observing the ground around it with the magnifying
  glass. Even a simple magnifying glass can reveal all kinds of beautiful,
  curious or bizarre creatures.

• *Blindfold hike*: Blindfold your children and lead them to a spot not too
  far from your starting point. Ask them to explore this spot with their

hands, noses and ears until they know the spot well. When they are
happy, take them back to the starting point and remove the blindfold.
The aim of the game is for them to use their non-visual observations to
identify the spot they explored.

- *Bird calling*: This is particularly appropriate since St Francis was
  renowned as a lover of birds. It is not necessary to spend hours patiently
  waiting for birds to put in an appearance. Many species will respond to
  simple calls out of sheer curiosity. One such call is a series of rhythmic
  'psssh' sounds. Try experimenting with different patterns for periods of
  a few seconds each. If you are self-conscious about making such noises,
  you can buy tapes of birdsong. Playing one of these on a portable
  recorder may well get the desired reaction.

  Obviously this will not work if you are crashing noisily through
  undergrowth in brightly coloured clothes. Wear something fairly plain
  and choose a spot in a wood where you can hear birds. Kneel or stand
  motionless for a few minutes before beginning to call. Usually birds in
  your vicinity will begin to respond quite rapidly.

- *Still hunting*: As the name suggests, this is simply a matter of finding a
  likely spot in a wood or on a hillside and staying still. Try to be as
  unobtrusive as possible, just a part of the natural surroundings,
  allowing the insects, birds and animals to go about their normal
  business.

  Most of us are simply too busy to appreciate the wonder of God's
  creation. An exercise like this allows us to slow down sufficiently to
  become much more aware of the natural world around us.

The wolf of Gubbio

This is one of many amazing stories told about St Francis. Modern readers
may find it hard to believe but it does highlight his love of peace and his
love of nature. It is sometimes suggested that it is a mythological account
of his visit to Sultan Melek-el-Kamal. Sadly his efforts to make peace
between the Sultan and the Crusaders besieging Damietta were less
successful than his encounter with the wolf.

> Once, when Francis was staying in Gubbio, a huge wolf began to
> terrorize the surrounding countryside. Everyone was terrified of the
> beast.
>
> Francis decided that something must be done about it, so he set off
> to talk to the wolf. Naturally the townspeople tried to stop him.

They told him how fierce the wolf was and begged him not to go. But his mind was made up.

Off he went, followed by a great crowd carrying knives and axes and cudgels, determined to protect Francis from himself. When he approached the wolf's lair it charged at him. He simply stood his ground, crying out, 'Brother Wolf! In the name of Christ I command you not to attack me or anyone else.' To the crowd's amazement, the wolf came and lay at Francis' feet like a pet hound. Then Francis reprimanded the wolf for terrorizing the people.

In response to Francis' pleas, the people of Gubbio agreed to welcome the wolf and feed it every day. The legend concludes by telling how the wolf lived peacefully in Gubbio until its death a couple of years later.

Reading: Ps. 104
Songs: 'All creatures of our God and King' (AMNS 105, MP 7)
        'If I were a butterfly' (JP 94, SOF 208)
        'Make me a channel of your peace' (MP 161, MP 456, SOF 381)
Prayer: 'May the power of your love, Lord Christ
        fiery and sweet as honey,
        so absorb our hearts that we may be ready
        to die for love of your love
        as you died for love of our love.'

(St Francis)

ST LUKE (18th October)

Caring for the sick is an integral part of Christian service. Jesus' own ministry was characterized by healing miracles and he sent his disciples out to 'heal the sick . . . and tell them "The kingdom of God is near you"' (Luke 10.9). Since St Luke is traditionally thought of as a doctor (thanks to Col. 4.14), his festival is a very appropriate time to recall this aspect of our faith.

Most of us know people who are unwell. This would be a good day on which to remember some of them. Why not go as a family to visit someone who is housebound? Or send someone a get well card?

In our culture, flowers are a traditional gift for someone who is ill. If you are interested in flower arrangement, why not give some thought to the theme of healing? Perhaps you could illustrate it by contrasting stark, violent colours (representing pain) with gentle greens, creams and pastel shades (representing peace).

This would be a good time to review your family's commitment to caring for others. What practical steps could you take to show more clearly that your faith is good news for those who are not whole in body or mind? Perhaps you could join a pastoral visiting rota at your local church. Why not find some way of supporting your local hospital, health centre or hospice?

Reading:	Luke 8.40–56
Songs:	'A man there lived in Galilee' (AMNS 334)
	'Dear Lord and Father of mankind' (AMNS 115, JP 37, MP 111, SOF 79)
	'Peace I give to you' (JP 196, MP 553)
	'Peter and John went to pray' (JP 198, MP 598)
	'When I needed a neighbour' (AMNS 433)
Prayer:	'Lord Jesus, bless those you have called to share in your ministry of healing. Give them skill, understanding and compassion. And help them to rely on you in all that they do. Amen.'

ONE WORLD WEEK

This is a recent addition to the churches' year, having started as an experiment in 1978. The Churches' Committee of the World Development Movement was looking for a way of making church members more aware of the world we live in and particularly issues relating to justice, peace and the environment. Their experiment was so successful that it now takes place annually in October.

Resources

The precise theme of One World Week varies from year to year. Details of each year's theme may be obtained from the One World Week Office, PO Box 100, London, SE1 7RT. They also supply a study/action guide for the current year.

Getting to know your world

You could use this week to focus on a specific country. Use your local library to find out more about it: its language, culture, religions, politics, economics, etc. Some missionary societies and development agencies may also be able to help (e.g. Tear Fund produces fact sheets on a number of developing countries).

Frugal meals

One practical way of taking One World Week seriously might be to have a frugal meal (or fast) each day during the week. Even something very simple by western standards (e.g. bread and soup) would be regarded as an ample meal in many developing countries. Why not collect the money saved during the week and donate it to a development charity such as Oxfam, Tear Fund or CAFOD?

Setting: Why not use a globe of the world as the centrepiece for your prayer corner this week? If you like, you could make it the centre of a flower arrangement including seasonal blooms and seed heads.

Songs: 'All over the world' (JP 5, MP 18, SOF 12)
'All people that on earth do dwell' (AMNS 100, JP 4, MP 20, SOF 13)
'Bind us together' (JP 17, MP 54, SOF 43)
'Eternal Ruler of the ceaseless round' (AMNS 353)
'God is working his purpose out' (JP 57, MP 189, SOF 135)
'Jesus shall reign where'er the sun' (AMNS 143, MP 379, SOF 301)
Or, to give your prayers an international flavour, you could experiment with songs from churches around the world. The Wild Goose Worship Group has recorded a cassette of such songs, called Many and Great and there is a music book to accompany it.

Prayers: Why not contact a Christian development agency or missionary organization for prayer suggestions this week?

ALL SAINTS (31st October/1st November)

Hallowe'en

Holding a festival at this time of the year is a custom dating back to before Christian times. Both the Romans and the Celts celebrated such festivals. In pagan Britain, 31st October was *Samhain*: a combination of New Year's Eve (since their calendar began with November) and a harvest festival. Fires were lit in preparation for winter and surplus livestock was slaughtered. Perhaps because it was a transition from one year to the next it was invested with supernatural significance: the spirits of the dead were believed to return. Thus offerings of food were made to placate the ancestors while fire and other devices (such as throwing nuts on the fire to create small explosions) were used to scare away evil spirits.

Similarly the Romans celebrated *Feralia* (the feast of the dead) and *Pomonia* (a feast in honour of the goddess of fruit) at about this time.

All Saints

This is an increasingly important festival for Christian families for the simple reason that, like St Valentine's Day, it is also an important secular festival: Hallowe'en. Unless you are part of the small minority of parents who send their children to a Christian school, your children will probably spend the best part of October involved in projects, plays and other activities about witches, ghosts and evil spirits. And even those children who are protected from Hallowe'en at school are likely to encounter it through contact with other children or references on television and radio.

With the revival of interest in occultism some of the pre-Christian pagan significance of Hallowe'en has been restored. This clearly raises important questions for Christian parents. How should we respond to such practices? Many Christians quite rightly feel uncomfortable about involvement in activities which either celebrate the occult or trivialize the supernatural. Should they merely condemn them and risk being seen as kill-joys or religious cranks?

We would like to suggest that the Christian festival of All Saints can be a constructive alternative. Indeed it has been a regular part of the liturgical calendar since the ninth century precisely to offer such an alternative. Like Valentine's Day it is a Christianization of a pre-Christian festival. Indeed the name Hallowe'en reflects that: it is the Eve of All Hallows (or All Saints).

For Christians it can be a day on which we remember all those who have gone before us in the faith. We celebrate all saints – all the people of God – not just the minority officially canonized by this church or that. We do not pray to or for them but remember that with them we are all part of the Church Universal.

Hallowe'en traditions

- *Bonfires*: Bonfires were lit at Hallowe'en to drive away evil spirits. But they also served a number of practical purposes. Most important was the burning of the debris of autumn. It also marked the onset of the winter months: at least some of the fires lit on Hallowe'en would be kept burning continuously until the spring, both for warmth and as a reminder that spring would come again.

- *Lanterns*: Daytime legal restrictions may mean that bonfires are a problem. But another tradition is to carve lanterns from turnips or pumpkins. These are often grotesque or macabre to reflect the sinister connotations of the season. But, since light is an important part of Christian tradition (not least because Christ is the Light of the world), Christians may want to reclaim this tradition for their own All Saints' celebrations. For example, friends of ours carve their pumpkin with a smiling face on one side and a fish on the other.

An alternative for younger children is to cut holes in a sheet of paper (in the shape of Christian symbols such as the fish or the cross) and then wrap the paper round a jam jar containing a candle.

Yet another possibility using a jam jar would be to wrap a paper-chain of saints around the jar. This chain can be made in just the same way as the chain of angels described earlier.

- *Food*: Hallowe'en was a traditional time for feasting because of its connection with the slaughtering of animals for winter. Today sausages and beans around the bonfire is a good family substitute for the traditional Hallowe'en feast. We also have a cake with a halo of candles on top (recalling the halo which is so often seen in medieval paintings of saints).

  It was also customary to bake soul cakes. Originally intended as an offering for the dead, these became a form of charity under Christian influence. The cakes were distributed to the poor. In later times fruit, nuts, sweets, beer or small amounts of money tended to be substituted for cake.

- *Trick or treat*: This is an increasingly important part of British Hallowe'en celebrations. The 'trick or treat' element is an American import which has been grafted on to the old custom of guising.

  In the form Lawrence remembers from his own childhood in Scotland, guisers were bands of children who would dress up and go from door to door entertaining the householders on Hallowe'en. In return for singing a song or reciting a poem, the children would receive small gifts of fruit, nuts or sweets. Perhaps it was a peculiarity of the west of Scotland, but there was relatively little emphasis on the macabre in the dressing up. Costumes were very diverse (on one occasion, for example, Lawrence dressed up as a Mexican peasant complete with jelly-bag sombrero and a shoe polish moustache).

  If your children cannot be dissuaded from the custom of 'trick or treat' it may be worthwhile trying to channel them in this more positive direction. Under parental supervision, the old custom of guising may be used to bring some pleasure to old and lonely people at Hallowe'en in contrast to the fear and anxiety sometimes created by 'trick or treat'. But be sure to let them know in advance that you are coming so that they will be prepared!

- *Bobbing for apples*: This traditional Hallowe'en game consists of attempting to take a bite out of an apple that is either floating in a basin of water or hanging from a string. Apparently, it was once believed that successfully biting the apple was a portent of good fortune in the coming year, but the game itself can easily be detached from that particular superstition. On its own, it is a harmless traditional piece of fun to enjoy with your children at this time of year.

All Saints activities

- *All Saints party*: Why not hold a party on Hallowe'en emphasizing the aspects of light and the communion of saints rather than darkness and the occult? As we have indicated above, many of the traditional Hallowe'en games and activities may be adapted for our use.

- *Stained glass saints*: Children can have fun creating their own stained glass windows from the acetate sheets used on overhead projectors. The outline of the saint may be drawn on to the sheet using a permanent marker pen. These outlines can be coloured in using water-based pens, or coloured tissue paper can be cut out and glued to the acetate using clear glue.

- *Saints charades*: The traditional game of charades can be adapted as a party game for All Saints. In this variation, the players each choose a saint or Bible character and try to convey the character's name without speaking.

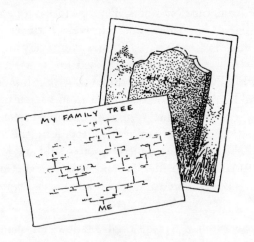

Dealing with death

In the western liturgical tradition the festival of All Saints was followed immediately by All Souls (on 2nd November). This allowed Christians to pay particular attention to one of the main features of the pagan autumnal festivals: death. It was a time for remembering the dead and, by implication, contemplating one's own mortality.

- *A book of remembrance*: Some churches maintain a book of remembrance containing the names of deceased parishioners. In some places these are read out as part of an All Souls' Day service. At one time, individual families might maintain a similar record of deceased relatives (often on the flyleaf of the family Bible).

Why not begin such a book? It could be a record of deceased relatives, friends, neighbours, men and women who have had a profound influence on our lives. But, in addition to a bare record of the date of their death, we might include photographs, reminiscences, anecdotes and anything else which helps us to remember their lives.

We live in a highly mobile and rootless culture. Such a book can be one way of providing our family with the historical roots that so many people now lack. All Souls can become an annual occasion for casual genealogical research as we gradually build up a fuller picture of our families and where they have come from.

- *Telling stories*: One of the implications of our modern isolation from the natural world has been an insulation from natural processes such as death. In modern western society death often takes place apart from the community in the antiseptic regime of the modern hospital. We are so protected from death that we find it difficult to talk about the deceased. As a result, an important part of the grieving process is hindered. Our pagan and pre-modern Christian forebears had no such inhibitions.

  We might use All Souls as an occasion to remember those who have been dear to us; to look again at old photographs; to swap stories about our experiences with them. For example, our children might remember their godmother 'Aunty' Ros who died of cancer a couple of years ago; Angela still talks about her trips to the theatre with her, and they also have memories of the Good Friday activities and holiday clubs she used to run at church.

- *Thinking about our own death*: All Souls may also be a good time to think about our own death. We know, in theory, that death is inevitable. But how many of us have actually spent any time considering the implications? How many of us, conversely, live as though we will never die? Judging by the high percentage of the British population that has not bothered to take the elementary step of making a will, many of us simply have not faced the possibility of our own death.

  This need not be a morbid exercise. On the contrary, it can be extremely constructive. To begin with there are the practical issues: making or updating a will (so that those we leave behind are spared unnecessary difficulties at a time of grief) and making plans for our funeral (a Christian funeral can be a final very powerful testimony to our Christian faith). But thinking about the implications of our death can also have positive implications for our life. Why not explore these possibilities by writing our own obituary? What will people say about you after you are dead? What would you like them to say about you? Such considerations may lead you to re-examine your life goals and vision.

- *Children's books on death and dying*: Like other major transitions in family life, there are now a number of books available which help children come to terms with death. We can recommend:
  > Helen Caswell, *God is Always With Me* (Abingdon Press, 1989)
  > Marge Heegaard, *When Someone Very Special Dies* (Woodland Press, 1991)
  > Doris Stickney, *Water Bugs and Dragonflies – explaining death to children* (Mowbray, 1984)
  > Susan Varley, *Badger's Parting Gifts* (Random Century, 1992)
  > Hans Wilhelm, *I'll Always Love You* (Hodder, 1985)

  For older children, you might try:
  > Rosa Guy, *The Friends* (Puffin, 1977)
  > Geraldine Kaye, *Comfort Herself* (Mammoth, 1990)
  > Jean Little, *Mama's Going to Buy You a Mockingbird* (Puffin, 1984)
  > E. B. White, *Charlotte's Webb* (Puffin, 1963)

  A book which may be suitable for teenagers is
  > Margaret Craven, *I Heard the Owl Call My Name* (Picador, 1976).

- *Other resources for thinking about death*: There is a vast literature on death, bereavement and grieving. One or two books that we have found helpful include:
  > Michael Hollings and Etta Gullick, *Prayers Before and After Bereavement* (Mayhew McCrimmon, 1985)
  > Jean Richardson, *A Death in the Family* (Lion, 1979)
  > Elaine Storkey, *Losing a Child: Finding a path through the pain* (Lion, 1989)

Music for All Saints and All Souls

Brahms	*A German Requiem*
Britten	*War Requiem*
Elgar	*Cello Concerto*

Fauré	*Requiem*
Honegger	*3rd Symphony (Liturgical)*
Mozart	*Requiem*
Tchaikovsky	*6th Symphony (Pathétique)*
Vaughan Williams	*Sinfonia Antarctica*
Eric Clapton	'Tears in Heaven' from *Eric Clapton Unplugged*
REM	'Everybody Hurts' from *Automatic for the People*

Thinking about heaven

For Christians, life eternal is the corollary of death. Instead of focusing on our mortality we might choose to think about our future life in Christ Jesus. What will it be like?

One or two of the books for younger children mentioned above look beyond death to the transformation promised in Christ. (Helen Caswell, for example, uses the metamorphosis of caterpillars into butterflies to explain death.) C. S. Lewis also tried to give us pictures of what heaven might be like. Perhaps either *The Last Battle* or *The Great Divorce* could be family reading at about this time of year.

ST ANDREW (30th November)

The missionary saint

In John's Gospel we are told that Andrew introduced his brother Peter to Jesus (John 1.40–42). For this reason, he is particularly associated with Christian missionary activity. Many churches have adopted the Sunday nearest St Andrew's Day as Missionary Sunday.

Why not use this day to reflect on your own commitment to the Church's mission? It is a good time to review your support for specific missions and missionaries and to pray for their work.

Andrew the fisherman

Like his brother, Andrew was a fisherman. This is a useful theme to pick up for family activities since Jesus himself likened mission to fishing (Mark 1.17). (See the notes on St Peter in Chapter 7 for ideas relating to this theme.) Another very simple way of picking up the theme would be to have fish as the main course of a family meal today.

The patron saint of Scotland

Families with Scottish connections (such as ours) may like to bring out this theme in their celebrations.

- *St Andrew's cross*: The flag of Scotland is St Andrew's cross. This is a white saltire cross (symbolizing purity) on a blue background (symbolizing the sea and again recalling that he was a fisherman). This is very easy for children to make. It can be drawn on a sheet of white paper, using blue felt-tip pens. Or it can be made from a sheet of overhead projector acetate using the technique described above for stained glass saints.

- *Shortbread*: This is easy to make and lends a Scottish flavour to your meal on St Andrew's Day.

    4 oz (115 g) butter, softened until creamy
    2 oz (50 g) raw brown sugar
    6 oz (170 g) wholemeal flour

Beat the butter with a wooden spoon. Add the sugar and beat it in. Sift the flour and add it, together with any bran that won't go through the sieve. Knead the dough briefly and pat it into a buttered 7-inch round tin. Mark out 6 or 8 portions and prick over with a fork. Bake for 45 minutes in an oven pre-heated to 150°C (Gas Mark 2).

Reading: John 6.1–15. This is the story of Jesus feeding the five thousand. Since most children enjoy improvising, why not act it out? If you feel the need of a script, you might look at the version in *The Dramatized Bible* (HarperCollins, 1989).

        Alternatively, there is a very amusing monologue written by John Bell and Graham Maule of the Iona Community ('The Majic Playpiece' in *Wild Goose Prints No. 1* (Wild Goose Publications, 1986) which looks at the story from the perspective of the boy who offered Jesus his packed lunch. (We first saw it being performed by a large American bishop dressed in shorts for the occasion!)

Songs: 'I will make you fishers of men' (JP 123)
              'Jesus calls us' (AMNS 312, MP 359)

9
Every Year

BIRTHDAYS

Family birthdays are annual events but, since they focus mainly upon growth and development, they are more appropriately dealt with under the pilgrimage of life rather than the cycle of the seasons. We may well have particular family traditions which recur every birthday but the emphasis is on change. That much is clear from the practice of giving birthday presents: the person whose birthday it is receives something (perhaps, many things) new.

Adults may sometimes prefer to play down their birthdays, but for most children they are very important. In childhood changes can take place with surprising rapidity. Sometimes those changes can be disturbing. A properly celebrated birthday recognizes and affirms these changes. It tells the child that, in the midst of these changes, he or she is an important person within the family.

Intangible presents

Present giving is an important part of birthdays. In our materialistic culture we are tempted to see this in entirely material terms. Television advertising, attractive displays in shops and the possessions of their friends encourage our children to compile (sometimes quite unrealistic) lists of what they would like for their birthday: things, things, things . . .

And yet sometimes the most important presents are the intangible ones. With each birthday we celebrate another year of life: a year which may bring new privileges and new responsibilities.

It is traditional to associate birthdays with increases in pocket-money and later bedtimes. A particular birthday may mean that the child is now old enough to join a club that he or she would like to be part of (e.g. a local uniformed organization). We may decide that they are now old enough to walk to school on their own, or ride their bikes without parental supervision, or have their own front door key. Most birthdays are likely to have some such privilege associated with them. We may wish to highlight this by issuing the child with a certificate to that effect!

Our culture puts a lot of emphasis on individual rights but tends to overlook the fact that every right has its attendant duties. This is something we may wish to stress by making birthdays the point at which a child takes on new responsibilities within the family as well as receiving new privileges. For example, they may be expected to tackle an additional household chore. Or it may be something more substantial: some friends of ours marked their teenage daughter's recent birthday by switching from pocket-money to a very much larger monthly allowance. But she is now expected to budget for her own cosmetics, sweets, magazines, etc. By gradually increasing their responsibilities we are also preparing our children for the day when they leave home and have to fend entirely for themselves.

Home-made cards and presents

Where possible, we encourage our children to make presents or cards rather than buy them. There is a personal dimension to such things which is lacking in their commercial counterparts. A home-made present may be less well-finished than something you might buy, but it is a gift of your time and your self rather than merely your money.

Related to this is an idea which was inspired by the example of Jackie Kennedy. What kind of birthday present could you find for a man with the

wealth and power of President Kennedy? Her answer was to get the
children to memorize and recite his favourite poems. Why not do the
same? Alternatively, you or members of your family could memorize and
perform a song or piece of music.

Birthday parties?

Parties are almost as traditional as presents but we suspect that many
parents are beginning to look forward to their children's birthday parties
with some apprehension. Our experience of life in middle-class parts of
England suggests that birthday parties are becoming increasingly commercial and linked to status. Keeping up with the Joneses may now include
booking the local sports centre/swimming pool/wildlife centre for an
expensive, professionally planned and supervised theme party.

But what messages do such parties convey to the children? Do they
perhaps suggest (along with expensive presents) that the importance of
people can be measured in purely financial terms? Does the child whose
birthday it is perhaps get overlooked as everyone concentrates upon the
excitement of the party? And could this suggest that the family's status (as
demonstrated by the party) is more important than the individual child?
Alternatively, might the child feel that his or her parents are too busy to
organize the party themselves – that they would rather buy a ready-made
party than waste their precious time on their child?

Judging by our own children's reactions to some of these parties, we
wonder to what extent the person whose birthday it is is really the centre
of attention. All the talk is about the activities, the food and the party
bags. Different parties are compared. And the child at the centre of it all is
often forgotten entirely.

We are not suggesting that parties should be banned! Far from it. But
we do think that it is a good idea to look seriously at our motives for
putting on an extravagant party or for handing over responsibility to
someone outside the family. Is it a question of status? Or busyness? Or do
we feel inadequate to plan and execute the kind of party our children
increasingly seem to expect? Having taken an honest look at our motives,
we may choose to do things differently.

Alternative party ideas

It is quite possible to turn a party into a memorable event without
resorting to buying an expensive professionally planned extravaganza.
Here are one or two ideas which have proved successful.

- *Pizza parties*: These have proved tremendously popular with our eldest daughter and her friends. We provide the pizza bases and raw materials for the toppings. They make the pizzas to their own specifications.

- *Pancake parties*: This is simply an extension of the previous idea. We tend to associate pancakes with Shrove Tuesday but there is no reason why we shouldn't eat them at other times. Pancake tossing is tremendous fun (provided you are prepared to tolerate a degree of mess in your kitchen) and pancakes are extremely versatile. Here is our recipe for a curried chicken pancake filling.

  > 1 medium onion (finely chopped)
  > 1 oz (30 g) butter
  > 12 oz (340 g) left-over chicken
  > $\frac{1}{2}$ tbsp curry powder
  > $\frac{1}{2}$ pint (285 ml) chicken stock
  > 1 apple (cored and chopped)
  > $\frac{1}{2}$ oz (15 g) sultanas
  > 2 slices lemon

  Fry the onion gently in the butter. Add the chicken and the curry powder and cook for five minutes, stirring frequently.

  Mix in the flour and gradually stir in the stock. Bring the mixture to the boil. Add the remaining ingredients and simmer for twenty minutes.

  This is sufficient for eight substantial pancakes.

- *Other DIY foods*: The above idea could be extended to other foods. Why not let them bake their own biscuits, or pop their own popcorn?

- *Creative party games*: Party games need not all be silly. Why not introduce the participants to some creative activity with which you are familiar? It might be candlemaking or soft toy making.

- *Theme parties*: These are always popular and, with an appropriate choice of theme, can be adapted to any age of partygoer.

  For younger children, a perennial favourite is the Teddy Bears' Picnic to which everyone brings their favourite soft toys. A variation on this is the Pooh party to which people can bring Winnie-the-Pooh and his friends. On such occasions, we have shown Winnie-the-Pooh videos or arranged readings of Pooh stories. Honey sandwiches are a compulsory part of the menu, of course! One memorable Pooh party that our children attended also included on the menu iced gems (Piglet's 'haycorns') and twiglets (Eeyore's thistles).

  Fancy dress parties (perhaps based on a particular historical period) are always popular. The keynote is to keep it simple. Instead of warning parents in advance you could tell the children the theme when they have arrived and provide them with simple materials from which to create their own costumes.

Yet another possibility (particularly for older children or teenagers) would be to choose another culture as the theme. Thus a dining room could be transformed into an Italian restaurant or a French bistro. The right atmosphere can be created by using a few simple props, e.g. a checked tablecloth, drippy candles in wine bottles. Why not visit your local library and find out a bit more about some of the customs associated with meals in the culture you have chosen? Perhaps your research could be the basis of a quiz or trivia game about the country in question.

If your family and their friends tend to be adventurous eaters you might venture further abroad: Greece, the Middle East, an Indian banquet or a Chinese dinner. Again the props can be relatively simple. One mum turned her living room into a bedouin tent by hanging blankets around the walls (in front of bookcases and display cabinets), removing the rest of the furniture and serving up a Middle Eastern supper (of pitta bread with various fillings) to her family as they sat on floor cushions. A Far Eastern atmosphere could be created by seating people at coffee tables and providing them with bowls and chopsticks!

A family celebration

Birthdays are first and foremost family celebrations. They are ways of affirming the individual's place within the family. In effect, by celebrating a birthday, we are saying 'this person is special to us'. Here are some ideas for making the birthday person the centre of the day:

- A *birthday banner*: Why not get the other family members to construct a banner to celebrate the birthday? This could be a large sheet of paper or card bearing the person's name. It may be decorated with bright colours and pictures or symbols indicating achievements or important mile-stones during the preceding year. Alternatively, you could construct a more permanent banner in the manner suggested in Chapter 1. Appropriate symbols could be added year by year, gradually building up into a pictorial record of the person's life within the family. When it is complete, hang it in a prominent position to announce to everyone who visits the house that it is N's birthday.

- *The birthday cake*: By tradition, birthday cakes announce the name of the birthday person and their age. But why not extend the banner idea to the cake? When the cake is iced you could include in the decorations some reference to the person's achievements or interests.

  Some years ago, we were members of a Christian community and such cakes were a regular feature of community birthday parties. For example, the year Lawrence had his first book published the community created a cake in the shape of a book for his birthday.

- *Outings and treats*: Why not ask the person whose birthday it is to choose a special treat for the day? Clearly it is not always practical to do what the child has chosen on his or her birthday: it may require too much time or planning. If so the treat could be deferred until a later date.

  A related possibility would be to take the birthday person on a magical mystery tour. Try to surprise them with a visit to a place or event that you know they will enjoy.

- *Family dinner*: Make it special and different. Use the best china and make the birthday person the guest of honour. The menu should consist of his or her favourite food (or items that he/she has specifically requested).

If the idea of a theme party, suggested above, is too much for you, why not give the family dinner a special theme? For example, for her birthday dinner this year our eldest daughter has requested a Chinese meal (we are already practising with our chopsticks!).

- *King (queen) for a day*: This is essentially an extension of the guest of honour idea which may appeal particularly to younger children. As soon as they get up they are crowned king or queen for the day (you can use a paper crown saved from Christmas or made for the occasion). For that day they are exempt from all their usual household chores and are generally treated as visiting royalty.

Birthdays and God

On birthdays family prayer times might well focus on the fact that this individual is important to God as well as to the rest of the family.

Instead of following your usual pattern of readings or stories you might like to choose one of the following Bible passages (or some other reading with a similar theme): Ps. 139.13–16; Isa. 43, 49.1; Jer. 1.4–10, 29.11; Rom. 5.8; Eph. 1.4–6; 1 Pet. 1.18–19; 1 John 3.1.

If songs or other kinds of music feature prominently in your family worship, you might consult the birthday person about what they would like. Similarly our prayers, too, may make a special mention of the person whose birthday is being celebrated. Here are some examples which may be used or adapted for family birthdays.

Heavenly Father, we thank you for the birthday of N and for all he/she means to us. Draw him/her closer to yourself each day, and draw us all closer together in your love. Amen.

Lord, we thank you for N's birthday. As we all grow in age help us also to grow in the knowledge of your love and become more like you. Amen.

Father, we thank you that you knew each of us before we were even formed. Thank you for making each of us unique. Thank you especially for the special person that you have created N to be. Help him/her always to remember this and that you will always be with him/her. Amen.

WEDDING ANNIVERSARIES

In spite of cultural pressures on family life, it is a simple fact that the majority of families follow the nuclear pattern. Every married couple is the nucleus of a separate family. The commitment to a common life which is made at marriage (or its secular equivalents) is what creates a family.

Thus wedding anniversaries should be an important part of family life. They recall and celebrate the commitment that lies at the heart of the family. In a sense they are analogous to birthdays: the birthday of the family. It is the commitment that makes the family, not the presence of children. A childless couple is no less a family than we are, with three children. We were a family for three years before our first child was born and we shall continue to be a family after the last child has left home.

On or about our wedding anniversary we usually take the opportunity to look back at our wedding day. We enjoy the photographs and other records of that day. More importantly we think about the promises we made on that day.

Likening anniversaries to birthdays, however, reminds us that there is more to them than fond remembrance of the past. Anniversaries should not be just nostalgia trips. They are also a time for celebrating the way the family has grown since those early days (and not just numerically): time for giving thanks for what has already happened and looking forward to what lies ahead.

From time to time it may be appropriate to recommit ourselves to the common life of the marriage vows. This may be an informal act or more formal before witnesses. Many couples, for example, choose to celebrate their silver wedding anniversary with a formal act of rededication in church. But why wait twenty-five years?

This is not to imply that such occasions should be solemn. On the contrary, they are a good excuse for a celebration. Some friends of ours celebrate their wedding anniversaries by inviting numbers of friends out for a meal. For their tenth anniversary they hired a church hall and packed it with friends.

Festive napkin rings

It is very easy to create your own napkin rings for a special celebratory dinner. All you need are some cardboard rolls at least 4.5 cm in diameter (from kitchen rolls or toilet rolls) and one or two other simple materials.

---

1. Make the appropriate number of rings by cutting 4 cm lengths off the end of the cardboard roll using a sharp knife.
2. Cut a piece of foil paper (6.5 cm by 15.5 cm). Paste the paper side of the foil with Copydex adhesive and insert into the ring, leaving about 1 cm protruding at either end.
3. Snip the protruding edges and turn over to secure.
4. Cut a piece of felt (4 cm by 15 cm) and stick to the outside of the ring.
5. Cut 2 pieces of braid (or very narrow ribbon) and stick to the outside edges of the ring. Complete the decoration with beads, sequins, small silk flowers, tinsel leaves, etc.

Welcome tree

This is a floral project for special occasions such as wedding anniversaries. To make it, you will need a green flowerpot, polyfilla, a wooden pole, a plant pot holder and a piece of oasis.

Fill the flowerpot with polyfilla and insert the pole before it sets. When dry the polyfilla can be hidden by a circle of green card or felt.

Nail the plant pot holder to the top of the pole. You may prefer to nail a circle of wood to the pole and tape the pot holder to that. The oasis is placed inside the holder and flowers appropriate to the occasion inserted into it. Finishing touches might include ribbons or trailing plants.

A friend of ours made one of these poles as a Christmas decoration last year. She used red spray carnations, gold chrysanthemums and winter jasmine with variegated ivy and periwinkle leaves. As a final touch, she filled the top of the flowerpot with sweets for visiting children.

THE SCHOOL YEAR

In our culture, school is a major feature of childhood and adolescence. The school year rather than the church year shapes their time with its pattern of term times and holidays. And because it shapes our children's years, it also shapes the time of every family with school-age children.

Most families take their holidays to coincide with school holidays. Many people move house or change jobs at times influenced by their children's schooling: moves are more likely to take place during holidays, the timing of job-hunting may be influenced by the stage of schooling their children have reached.

In spite of its importance, the school year tends to be neglected by most families. Perhaps this is because it is something that happens 'out there' in the public arena: it is to children what the world of work is to adults. Precisely because it is public, many people in our culture tend to separate it off from the private world of family life. The closest most parents come to a ritual recognition of the importance of school is the annual spending spree before the beginning of the school year.

We can do a good deal to recognize and affirm the importance of school for family life. For example, we might pray regularly for the school and its work (in much the same way as we might pray for our place of work – and for much the same reasons). We can get some idea of what to pray for from our children but also through active involvement in the parents' association and getting to know any Christian teachers on the staff.

We can also devise ceremonies and traditions which give the school year a positive place in our family life. Like birthdays, although these will recur year after year for as long as children are at school, the emphasis is on change and development rather than on recurrence. Each new term brings new challenges, new disappointments, new achievements, new joys.

Affirming a new year/term

The new term might well be the central focus for family prayers on the evening before it begins. This is an opportunity to talk about our hopes and fears for the coming term (or year). Such a chance to talk may be particularly important if someone is about to begin a new school. Pray about those hopes and fears; don't forget to pray for the teachers too!

Some families might find it helpful to bless (or dedicate) the new school equipment and clothes which each child will be using in the coming term. Why not ask each participant in family prayers to present an item symbolizing one aspect of schoolwork? As the supplies are piled up in front of you, use them as a visual aid to assist your prayers.

> 'God of love,
> Bless these children whom I/we love.
> Watch over them as they go to school.
> Open their minds to the knowledge that will be given them,
> And protect them in all their encounters.'

End of term

The end of each term is an opportunity to celebrate the achievements of the past term. Many schools still acknowledge the academic or sporting achievements of their pupils. In a family context, it may be more important to acknowledge and give thanks for some of the other achievements.

Perhaps some tangible recognition of these achievements might be appropriate. The school our children attend does not have a prize-giving ceremony so we have our own family prize-giving to mark particular achievements.

Clearly such celebrations have to be adapted to the ages of the children involved. Otherwise there may well come a time when the children are simply embarrassed by your rituals. However, with suitable modification, the formal recognition of beginnings and endings of terms can continue throughout school and university education. In doing so you are expressing the fact that what your children do at school and college is every bit as important for the life of the family as adult work.

10
Transitions in the Family

Families are dynamic, living realities. They are constantly changing as the members grow and change. Thus it is not enough to celebrate the Christian year or even the recurring festivals of family life. We also need to affirm in our family celebrations those changes which cannot be tied to particular dates or seasons. These include what anthropologists call the rites of passage: the transition of family members from one stage of life to another. Such changes affect the family as a whole as well as the individual member.

ADDITIONS TO THE FAMILY

All changes in the number of people in a household alter its dynamics in some way. This is true whether the addition is a new baby, an adopted or fostered child, an elderly relative or a lodger. The suggestions we make here are focused primarily on the arrival of a new baby but it should be possible to adapt them to other similar situations.

Parents may well have spent months preparing for the new arrival. Older children will also have anticipated the arrival (perhaps with more mixed feelings than the parents). During this preparation time, existing children can be helped to understand some of the changes that are likely to take place. There are many children's books suitable for different ages which parents may use with their children.

But, however much you prepare and anticipate, it always falls short of the reality. A new baby changes the family routines quite dramatically. As we discovered, twins feeding and sleeping on completely different schedules can destroy those routines for weeks or even months. Such changes are often felt most acutely by other children who may feel neglected or unloved in the face of all the attention being lavished on the baby.

A number of books on family celebrations make suggestions about rituals for welcoming new family members. For example it may be appropriate to throw a party to celebrate. In the USA such parties often include a shower (friends and neighbours turn up with presents for mother and baby). To add a religious dimension, why not form a procession to the room which will be occupied by the baby? Once there you might have a short time of prayer giving thanks for mother and child and asking God's blessing on the whole family.

Procession: *with song:* 'He's got the whole world in his hands' (JP 78, MP 225)

Prayer: 'Creator God,
we praise you for the wonder and joy of all that you have made.
We give you thanks for the life of [*child's name*].
Help us to be trustworthy as her/his family and friends.
Give us patience, understanding and wisdom for the task of guiding [N] to maturity
through Jesus Christ our Lord. Amen.'

Reading: 'People were bringing little children to Jesus to have him touch them, but the disciples rebuked them. When Jesus saw this, he was indignant. He said to them, "Let the little children come to me, and do not hinder them, for the kingdom of God belongs to such as these. I tell you the truth, anyone who will not receive the kingdom of God like a little child will never enter it." And he took the children in his arms, put his hands on them and blessed them' (Mark 10.13–16).

Prayers: Those who are present may appreciate the opportunity to offer their own prayers.

Blessing: [*addressed to the child*]
'The Lord bless you and keep you;
the Lord make his face shine upon you and be gracious to you;
the Lord turn his face towards you and give you peace'
(Num. 6.24–26).

Any such act of welcome must, of course, take into account the feelings of other family members. It should certainly not make them feel marginal or unimportant. One way to counter this danger might be to use the occasion to celebrate increased responsibilities (and privileges) for older brothers and sisters. They may also be encouraged to be involved in the looking after of the baby. Perhaps they could keep the baby's clothes organized, or help with washing or feeding.

Welcoming an older person into family membership will, of course, be rather different. But there could still be a party or celebration. For an older person who is giving up some degree of independence it may be important to identify a clear role within the family: as family members rather than house guests or lodgers they may welcome some responsibility for the work that keeps the family functioning.

FORGIVING AND BEING FORGIVEN

It may seem strange to include reconciliation in a chapter on transitions in family life. However, it seems less strange when we recall that reconciliation invariably involves repentance; a radical change of direction, from death to life. This is one transition which, far from being occasional, should be a regular (if not daily) part of Christian family life.

Forgiveness is absolutely fundamental to the good news of Jesus Christ. He both proclaimed and made possible the restoration of relationships broken by human sin – our relationship with God but also our relationships with each other, with creation and with ourselves. We acknowledge the reality of our sinfulness and celebrate God's forgiveness in Jesus Christ every year in the annual cycle of Christian worship. Penitence and forgiveness are basic to Lent, Holy Week and Easter.

However, the need to forgive and be forgiven is also a daily reality for Christian families. Whenever we live in close proximity with one another, there is potential for offence to be given or taken. Christians who have been called to live in community often insist that it is not an easy option precisely for this reason.

Whenever we say the Lord's Prayer we recall the fundamental importance of penitence and forgiveness: 'Forgive us our sins as we forgive those who sin against us.' Failure to admit our own sins or forgive the sins of others is corrosive of personal relationships. That is why Jesus counselled people to put reconciliation before worship (Matt. 5.23–24): without reconciliation, acts of worship are empty words. It also explains his insistence on repeated forgiveness (Matt. 18.21–35): once you refuse to forgive you destroy a relationship.

In our own home, we tend to take Jesus' advice about forgiveness and worship fairly literally. Combining it with Paul's dictum, 'Do not let the sun go down while you are still angry' (Eph. 4.26), we try to settle the day's disagreements and offences before bedtime prayers.

Usually all that is required is a 'sorry' and an 'I forgive you'. However, you may find this inadequate for the occasional major family dispute. We spent a couple of years as members of a Christian community which had learned the necessity of a formal liturgy for reconciliation. If you discover that something more is needed, you might like to incorporate the act of forgiving and being forgiven into family prayers. The simple act of putting it in such a context is a reminder both of the importance of forgiveness and the reality of God's forgiveness which makes our forgiveness credible.

Reading: 'If we claim to be without sin, we deceive ourselves and the truth is not in us. If we confess our sins, he is faithful and just and will forgive us our sins and purify us from all unrighteousness' (1 John 1.8f).

Act of confession and forgiveness

Prayer: [*holding hands*] 'Lord, we thank you that you forgive us as we forgive one another. Grant us the grace to live in harmony with each other and in union with you. Amen.'

Song: 'God forgave my sin' (JP 54, MP 181, SOF 129)
          'He was pierced' (MP 222, SOF 173)
          'Jesu, lover of my soul' (AMNS 123, MP 372, SOF 297)
          'Love divine' (AMNS 131, MP 449, SOF 377)

MOVING HOME

We have been married twelve years. In that time we have moved house seven times. Between the ages of five and eleven Lawrence lived in four different places and attended eight different schools. A friend of ours in her late fifties has had over thirty different homes. At the school our children attend the teachers estimate that between thirty and fifty per cent of the children change each year. There is a similarly high turnover of families at our local parish church. Mobility is a fact of life for many people in our culture.

Mobility: in the words of Toad of Toad Hall, 'Here today – in next week tomorrow!' It is one of the factors which contributes to the dynamism and novelty of modern western culture. Economic necessities play their part, of course. Uncertainty about jobs, the possibility of promotion or greater security, the needs of multi-national employers all call for greater mobility. But it is driven by more than economics. It is also an integral part of modern culture. It is an opportunity for fresh beginnings; a chance to break free from the shackles of the past. But it is also a major cause of the rootlessness which afflicts so many people today.

Moving home is one of the common experiences of modern life. It is also reckoned to be one of the most traumatic, next only, in terms of stress, to the death of a close relative. In spite of the apparent homogeneity of modern life, moving from one town to another can cause culture shock: relationships are broken, all the services one takes for granted have to be rediscovered, you have to get used to shopping in new stores, to driving on new roads.

Sadly our churches have done little to recognize the importance of such experiences in the life of the family. As far as our liturgies and rituals are concerned we still live in a stable pre-industrial culture: they tend to assume that the norm is for people to be born, nurtured, married, to live their lives and die all in a single community. The reality is that today that is the rare exception rather than the norm. Thus we need to explore ways of celebrating such changes, ritual ways of enabling ourselves and our families to handle such changes.

Leaving

It is important to leave well. The temptation of our individualistic culture is to assume that moving house is a purely private affair. We inform close friends and relatives, we give our change of address to our bank, our employers and relevant government authorities. But the first that acquaintances at church know of it is the sight of an empty pew on Sunday. Too many people simply disappear.

However, if (as Christian theology suggests) we are never simply isolated individuals then our departure affects the entire comunity. Some years ago Lawrence had an acquintance who was involved in research for a multi-national computer firm. His employers asked him to move to Japan at a month's notice. They made sure all his financial liabilities were covered and even provided for members of his family. But at the end of that month the local church was left without one of its key youth leaders. Relationships were broken. One person's unexpected departure affected the entire church.

It is important to leave a community well. This is true whether you are the vicar or an ordinary member of the congregation. Because, as Christians, we are members of an extended family, the family of God, the Church, we should make our farewells to the entire family. Our last parish was quite adept at this kind of farewell – it was an opportunity for a communal Sunday lunch followed by farewells and appropriate entertainments (in our case a bouncy castle!). If such an event is not possible, the person or people leaving might ask to put a farewell letter in the parish magazine or church newsletter. This could include their new address and any requests for prayer. Some churches might consider devising a liturgy of leave-taking. John Westerhoff and William Willimon[1] suggest that such a liturgy should include some statement of why the family is moving, time for remembering some of the experiences the family has shared with the community, a scriptural meditation on the theme of pilgrimage and a concluding blessing/sending forth. A good example of a service of leave-taking is 'Praying our Farewells' in the Office Book of the Society of Saint Francis.[2] The following brief service of leave-taking follows a similar structure:

Going forth with God

Opening sentence:	' "I am the Alpha and the Omega," says the Lord God, "who is, and who was, and who is to come, the Almighty" ' (Rev. 1.8).
Prayer:	'God of our beginnings and endings, we celebrate all we have shared together and ask your blessing as they/we continue their/our journey. May your love unite us for ever. May the power of your presence bless this leave-taking; for the sake of Jesus Christ, our Redeemer. Amen.'
Readings:	One or more of Exod. 13.21–22; Ps. 139.1–3, 8–10; John 3.5–8; John 16.21–24; 2 Cor. 4.7–9; Phil. 1.3,4,9.
Inter-cessions:	A period for brief prayers asking God's blessing on those who are leaving; and that through this change of circumstances they will meet Christ in new ways and continue to grow spiritually. (It may be appropriate for those leaving to use a short response, e.g. 'I know that God goes with me.')
Blessing:	'God of the journey we give you thanks for N. We entrust them to your loving care. Shelter and protect them from all harm and anxiety. Grant them courage to meet the future, and grace to enter into new life; through Jesus Christ our Saviour. Amen.'
Song:	'I want to walk with Jesus Christ' (JP 124) 'Lead us, heavenly Father' (AMNS 224, MP 400, SOF 321) 'Through all the changing scenes of life' (AMNS 209, MP 702) 'We rest on thee' (MP 735, SOF 587) 'When the road is rough' (JP 279) 'Who would true valour see' (AMNS 212)
Peace	

Ideas for making leaving easier

As individual families we ought also to recognize the importance of leaving well. Adults and children alike may be very upset by a move from familiar surroundings and all their friends to some completely new situation. Within the family we need to recognize the trauma of leaving and provide opportunities for every family member to express and work through some of the feelings we have about a particular place.

- *Recalling the good and the bad*: One thing we have tried and found helpful has been to ask the children to draw pictures of good and bad experiences which they associate with a particular place or period. These pictures enable them to share some of the feelings they cannot express in words. When we did this before our most recent move it revealed that two of the children were still upset by an incident they had witnessed outside Kew Gardens. We were able to go back there and lay that particular ghost to rest before moving.

- *Family archaeology*: Archaeology is all about digging up the past. Plenty of that goes on when a family prepares to move house. The rubbish that has accumulated in cupboards is turned out and sifted. The contents of the attic are uncovered. Sooner or later old photographs or letters turn up. This is an opportunity for you to stop and recall old memories and experiences. As someone whose family has regularly done this comments, 'Suddenly we're no longer adrift. Our past nurtures and supports our family's future.'[3]

- A *farewell party*: A party can be a good way of saying goodbye. It allows the children to say farewell to their best friends in a positive way – far better than hasty farewells in the school playground.

- *Stories about moving on*: If reading is a regular part of family times together, this may be used to help children get used to the idea of moving house by looking at stories which involve moves from one place to another. Several of Laura Ingalls Wilder's classic *Little House on the Prairie* stories involve moving house as a recurring theme, as they recount her own childhood in an American pioneer family.

- *Family time together*: Preparing for a move is often a hectic time for parents. There are change of address cards to be posted, gas and electricity readings to be arranged, subscriptions to be cancelled; there are things to be sorted out and packed. It is only too easy to allow such busyness to crowd out time for each other.

At such times children can easily become insecure as the familiar features of the home gradually disappear into boxes. Though we are less likely to show it, adults too find the dismantling of their home very traumatic. It is important therefore that we should make time for each other. Perhaps we could have a special family dinner with all our favourite foods before the best crockery and cutlery is packed away. Or we might watch our favourite videos or play our favourite games one last time before they too disappear into boxes.

Arriving

Departures are the necessary precursor to arrivals. Every arrival is a new beginning. Again this is something which comes across clearly in the *Little House* stories.

New beginnings are theologically and spiritually important. Handled properly they are opportunities for greater intimacy with God. They are a chance to break with old habitual sins. Unfortunately they can also be times at which old relationships, including our relationship with God, are severed.

Thus how the Christian community welcomes newcomers is vitally important. Anonymous tranference of membership from one church to another is hopelessly inadequate. Some public recognition of their arrival is called for.[4] Similarly, in these days of extreme mobility, the local church cannot wait for people to settle in and volunteer their services.

Suggestions for arriving well

Equally important is how we view arrival ourselves.

- *Invite a friend*: We never break completely with our past. As we arrive in a new place it helps if some of our roots in our previous environment are nurtured. One clergy wife who has ample experience of moving recommends allowing the children to invite a friend or two to accompany them during the move and stay for a week or so at the new house.

  That may sound too much like hard work for hard-pressed parents facing the prospect of unpacking and rearranging all their furniture and belongings! When we last moved we adopted a more modest form of the idea: we invited friends from our previous home to visit us for the weekend after our move. It gave all of us (children and parents alike) something to look forward to; it also concentrated our minds wonderfully on the process of unpacking!

- *Family time together*: As with the period of uneasiness before a move, it is particularly important not to neglect time together afterwards.

  Take time off from the unpacking to explore your new locality. Parents might usefully plan outings which will enable them to 'discover' places or things which the children will enjoy.

  Catherine Cole comments of such times, 'I have come to treasure the closeness our family shares immediately after a move.'[5]

- *Resolutions for a new home*: It may help to identify and share our hopes and fears for our new home. Since a new home is an even more important fresh start than a new year it seems appropriate to turn some of these into resolutions about how life in our new home is going to differ from (and how it is going to remain the same as) life previously.

An act of dedication for the new home

Our resolutions might be incorporated into an act of worship dedicating the family and its new home to God. Again this is something for which Christian tradition provides few guidelines. One helpful source of ideas is the Iona Community with its liturgy for the opening of a Columban House (i.e. one of the communal homes of community members).[6]

| Opening sentence: | [*read at the front door*] 'Here I am! I stand at the door and knock. If anyone hears my voice and opens the door, I will come in and eat with him, and he with me' (Rev. 3.20). |

Prayer:	'Lord Jesus, be welcome in this home. Be present in all the living that will be done here. Grant that all who live here may demonstrate your love in their lives. Amen.'
Procession:	*The worshippers now move from room to room asking God's blessing on each room, the people who will use them and the activities that will take place there. The prayers may be extempore or adapted from traditional blessings (e.g. those of Celtic Christianity). A candle may be lit to signify Christ's presence in that room.*
Song:	'Lord of all hopefulness' (AMNS 394) 'The wise man built his house upon the rock' (JP 252)

Peace

The climax of the service could be a celebratory meal. Be sure to involve every family member in the act of worship. It would be appropriate to invite both old friends and new acquaintances to this celebration, recalling that in setting up a new home and establishing new relationships we are not simply abandoning former relationships.

LEAVING HOME

Sooner or later, children grow up and leave home. This is a time of change and, hence, stress for both the one who is leaving and those who stay behind. The stress is undoubtedly greatest when the departure is accompanied by recriminations, but even the happiest of departures may be stressful.

The one who is leaving is embarking on a new stage of his or her life. It may be college, or a new job, or marriage. All of these bring with them both hope and uncertainty.

For those staying behind, this departure means significant readjustments in the dynamics of the family. At a trivial level, younger brothers or sisters may be lining up to take over the vacant room. Adjustments have to be made to the roles and routines of the remaining family members. This may range from reallocating the vacuuming to the trauma of a surrogate parent leaving.

Children leaving home may be almost as traumatic as death or divorce (which, in a sense, are both extreme variations on the same theme – the dynamics of the family are disrupted because so-and-so who always did such-and-such is no longer there). All of these are the family equivalent of major surgery or amputation.

Indeed many couples separate or divorce shortly after the last child leaves home. This is particularly true of families which centred on the children. In such cases, the couples discover that they have become comparative strangers over the years. The change in the dynamics of the family is so great that they are simply unable to cope. Sometimes this results in the child whose departure has provoked the breakdown being overcome by guilt.

The trauma experienced by the family is one reason for seeking to leave well. Another reason is that genuine maturity and independence depend upon leaving well. It is sometimes said by family therapists that a man cannot really marry his wife until he has divorced his mother. We may physically leave home while remaining tied to our family by intangible bonds. In a later series of 'The Cosby Show', the son Theo has 'left home' in this way: he is now living some distance away but he has not ceased to be part of the family (he brings his washing home and seems to eat most of his meals there). Such a transitional phase may be acceptable for college students but it becomes unhealthy if it drags on very long. In such cases more drastic measures have to be taken. For example, we know of one young man in his twenties who had to emigrate to Australia to escape his mother!

What we have already said suggests that there is more to leaving home properly than packing one's bags. It may be worth taking time to think through as a family the implications of leaving and discuss ways in which the family might adjust to the departure. Take stock of the role the person plays within the family. What does he or she contribute to family life? Who is going to take on his or her chores? How are household routines to be adjusted to accommodate the changes?

A liturgy for leaving

Some families may find it helpful to formalize the departure of a family member. This could involve the handing over of symbolic gifts: those staying could give appropriate gifts to the one departing (e.g. a new suitcase or domestic items for a new flat). The one who is leaving may like to symbolize the responsibilities he or she is handing over to other family members (if it was the washing up, perhaps a pair of rubber gloves – symbols need not always be deadly serious, and family rituals can be fun). This may well be a good time for parents to hand over personal papers which they have hitherto been responsible for, such as passport, birth certificate, insurance policy documents, savings account books. Such an act is a visible sign that you are giving that person their independence.

Christian parents may well want to do this in the context of an act of worship. One possible pattern might be as follows.

Reading: Gen. 12.1–4 (or another appropriate reading on the theme of pilgrimage to a new land)

Thanksgiving: Take time to reflect on your life together (perhaps using photographs, videos or other mementoes); thank God for the time he has given you together.

Presentation   Gifts are given and received, perhaps with a brief
of gifts: statement of their significance (e.g. 'We bring you soap, so that you might never be afraid to get your hands dirty in the service of your neighbour.')[7]

This may be incorporated into the service of leave-taking described earlier in the chapter.

A DEATH IN THE FAMILY

Death is the ultimate departure. However, since it is a traumatic experience for any family, it may be better to treat it in some other way than merely as and when it occurs. In western Christian traditions, All Saints and All Souls have been traditional times for thinking about death and remembering loved ones who have died. We have followed that tradition in this book and so various suggestions on handling death within the family will be found in Chapter 8.

NOTES

Chapter 1

1 M. Vasey et al., *Family Festivals* (Nottingham, Grove Books, 1980), p. 22.
2 Throughout this book we make suggestions of hymns and choruses that might be appropriate for different occasions. Wherever possible we have selected these songs from four popular hymn books:
   Hymns Ancient and Modern New Standard Version (AMNS)
   Cry Hosanna (CH)
   Junior Praise (JP)
   Mission Praise, combined edition (MP)
   Songs of Fellowship (1991 edition) (SOF)
   Sound of Living Waters (SOLW)
3 See Lawrence Osborn, *Paper Pilgrimage: Keeping a personal and spiritual journal* (London, DLT/Daybreak, 1990), pp. 42–46.

Chapter 3

1 Joanna Bogle, *A Book of Feasts and Seasons* (Leominster, Fowler Wright, 1988), p. 28.

Chapter 4

1 Joan Halmo, *Celebrating the Church Year with young children* (Collegeville, Minn., Liturgical Press, 1988), p. 78.
2 Halmo, *Celebrating the Church Year*, p. 76.

Chapter 5

1 Except were stated, they can be found in the National Gallery, London.
2 Formerly these were used instead of real palm fronds in English churches and are still sometimes called willow palm.
3 This song is particularly appropriate today because Maundy Thursday takes its name from the traditional anthem *Mandatum novum*: 'A new commandment' (John 13.34).
4 This can be found in *Enemy of Apathy: Wild Goose Songs, Vol 2* (Glasgow, The Iona Community, 1988). Many of the songs in this and the companion volumes are set to well-known British folk tunes.
5 See e.g. Martha Zimmerman's *Celebrate the Feasts* (Minneapolis, Bethany House, 1981), pp. 49–94, or (for a simpler version) Sandra DeGidio's *Enriching Faith*, pp. 72–86.

6 This chant can be found on more than one recording of Taizé worship. Like many Taizé chants it is easy to sing (or you might prefer to listen to a recording).

Chapter 6

1 Halmo, *Celebrating the Church Year*, p. 53.

Chapter 10

1 John H. Westerhoff III and William H. Willimon, *Liturgy and Learning Through the Life Cycle* (New York, Seabury Press, 1980), pp. 136–141.
2 *The Daily Office SSF: A version of Celebrating Common Prayer* (London, Mowbray, 1992), pp. 298–300.
3 Catherine Cole, 'Helping the family manage the move' in *Leadership*, Vol. 12 no. 2, 1991, p. 80.
4 e.g. 'A Litany for Reception of New Members' in *Bread for the Journey: Resources for Worship* edited by Ruth C. Duck (Cleveland, Ohio, Pilgrim Press, 1981), pp. 15–16. Alternatively the Iona Community's Welcome Liturgy might serve as a model: see *Iona Community Worship Book*, pp. 6–8.
5 Cole, 'Helping the family', p. 81.
6 *Iona Community Worship Book*, pp. 44–48.
7 Degidio, *Enriching Faith*, p. 107.

FURTHER RESOURCES

Bible stories

Pat Alexander, *The Lion Children's Bible* (Oxford: Lion, 1981)

Michael Forster, *A Story, A Hug and a Prayer: A Family Bedtime Book* (Bury St Edmunds: Kevin Mayhew, 1994)

Penny Frank, *The Lion Story Bible* (Oxford: Lion, 1985) [A collection of 52 short illustrated volumes]

Anne de Graaf, *Adventure Story Bible* (Swindon: Bible Society, 1991) [A collection of 30 short books retelling favourite Bible stories]

Andrew Knowles, *Fount Children's Bible* (London: Fount, 1986)

Palm Tree Bible Stories (Bury St Edmonds: Palm Tree Press, 1983)

Prayer

The Lion Book of Children's Prayers (Tring: Lion, 1977)

Jane Reehorst, *Guided Meditations for Children: How to Teach Children to Pray Using Scripture* (Dubuque, Iowa: Wm Brown, 1986)

Nancy Roth, *Praying: A Book for Children* (New York: Church Hymnal Corporation, 1991)

Deborah Roslak & Linda Joy Orber, *Dear Jesus, Dear Child: Guided Meditations for Young Children* (Mystic, CN: Twenty-Third Pubications, 1992)

Worship songs

The Big Book of Spring Harvest Kid's Praise (Eastbourne: ICC, no date)

Ishmael's Family Worship Songbook (Eastbourne: Kingsway, 1988)

Alan Price, *Shine Shine Shine* (Eastbourne: ICC, 1990)

Alan Price, *Salt and Light* (Eastbourne: ICC, 1992)

Worship . . . at HTB! (London: HTB Publications, no date)

Worship for Kids Songbook (Anaheim, CA: Vineyard Ministries International, 1989)

Christine Wright, *Let's Join In! A collection of action songs and rhymes* (London: Scripture Union, 1994)

Christine Wright, *Let's Praise and Pray: A collection of songs, rhymes and prayers* (London: Scripture Union, 1994)

General resources

Mary Batchelor, *The Lion Christmas Book* (Oxford: Lion, 1984)

Kathy Bence, *Turn off the TV: Let's have fun instead!* (London: Marshall Pickering, 1990)

Sandra DeGidio, *Enriching Faith through Family Celebrations* (Mystic, CT: Twenty-Third Publications, 1989)

Marjorie Freeman, *We Always Put a Candle in the Window: Celebrating Christian Festivals at Home* (London: Church House Publishing, 1989)

Joan Halmo, *Celebrating the Church Year with Young Children* (Collegeville, Minn.: Liturgical Press, 1988)

Ann Hibbard, *Family Celebrations: Meeting Christ in Your Holidays and Special Occasions* (Brentwood, TN: Wolgemuth & Hyatt, 1988)

Jane Keiller, *Praying with Children in the Home* (Nottingham: Grove Books, 1992)

Ian Knox, *. . . And All the Children Said Amen: Praying Together at Home* (London: Scripture Union, 1994)

Getrud Mueller Nelson, *To Dance With God: Family Ritual and Community Celebration* (New York: Paulist Press, 1986)

Pat & Rosemary Ryan, *Advent Begins at Home: Family Prayers and Activities* (Liguori, Missouri: Liguori Publications, 1979)

Pat & Rosemary Ryan, *Lent Begins at Home: Family Prayers and Activities* (Liguori, Missouri: Liguori Publications, 1978)

A Path Through Advent for Children; A Path Through Lent for Children; A Path Through Eastertide for Children (Southend: McCrimmon's) [three booklets of activities, prayers and reflections published annually]

Edith Schaeffer, *What is a Family?* (London: Hodder & Stoughton, 1978)

Michael Vasey et al., *Family Festivals* (Nottingham: Grove Books, 1980)